SOCIAL MACHINES

SOCIAL MACHINES

How to Develop Connected Products That Change Customers' Lives

PETER SEMMELHACK

WILEY

Library of Congress Cataloging-in-Publication Data:

Semmelhack, Peter, 1965-
    Social machines : how to develop connected products that change customers' lives /
Peter Semmelhack.
        pages cm
        Includes index.
        ISBN 978-1-118-47168-5 (cloth)
            1. Social media—Economic aspects. 2. Social networks. I. Title.
HM741.S46   2013
302.3—dc23
                                                                    2012050967

I dedicate this book to my wife, Suzanne, and children, Tristan and Victoria, my most important social network.

CONTENTS

ACKNOWLEDGMENTS

This book is the result of a journey I've been on for several years with many people and organizations. To all of my backers and supporters—financial, professional, personal, and otherwise—a sincere thank you. The material in these pages would have been impossible without you. To everyone I have worked with in bringing Bug Labs to life and through all its stages, this book has your collective fingerprints all over it. Thanks for everything you've contributed. Thanks to everyone at John Wiley & Sons, Inc., for giving me the chance to write my first book and providing a wonderful staff of editors and artists to support and guide me through it all.

Thanks to my family and friends for putting up with my frequent disappearances and silent treatments as I wrote. And finally, thank you to my wonderful wife and children for being my constant source of inspiration, motivation, and laughter.

PART I

Social Machines
An Overview

Machines take me by surprise with great frequency.
—*Alan Turing*

CHAPTER 1

Introduction

It was Saturday morning, and Melissa was making a stop at her local Walmart to pick up a few things. As usual, she parked as close as she could and walked the familiar pavement up to the well-lit store entrance. Upon entering, her eye was drawn to something unfamiliar in the lobby. Standing against what used to be an empty wall was now a large, colorful, slightly unusual-looking vending machine. Intrigued, Melissa approached it—and immediately noticed a couple of things. For one, the machine was completely stocked with only one product—bright green Cascade dishwashing detergent samples made by Procter & Gamble (P&G). Second, in place of the normal mechanism by which you would insert coins or bills to make a purchase, there was a large, rectangular, color LCD screen that welcomed her with the line, "Press here to get your free sample!" Her finger instinctively reached out and pressed the screen where instructed. The screen promptly displayed:

> Using your smartphone, please visit our product's Facebook page. After you log in, go to this URL— http://cascade.facebook.com.
> If you Like our page, we'll vend you a free sample of our new Cascade dishwashing detergent right here, right now!

Melissa was hooked. She retrieved her iPhone from her pocket . . . and paused. Was this strange new transaction worth it? By pressing that "Like" button, she would be telling all her Facebook friends that she, in fact, liked this promotion. After examining the machine some more and thinking about the companies involved, she pressed the "Like" button with her pinkie. Two seconds later the vending machine whirred and dropped a sample into the tray for her to pick up. Melissa let out a quick laugh, looked around to make sure it wasn't some kind of trick, and reached in to grab the sample. She would try it tonight, she decided, and noticing the coupon on the back of the packaging, pondered whether she might just pick up a whole box of it while shopping then and there.

Welcome to *social machines*, a world in which social networks include not just other *people* but Internet-connected electronic *devices*, *machines*, and *contraptions* of all kinds. It's a world where your next Twitter follower could be your refrigerator and your new Facebook friend your brother's Mustang. It is a *business ecosystem* of people, companies, and machines collaborating in surprising new ways and opening up innovative possibilities to create real value.

Let's examine all the people and groups that benefitted from this simple interaction at Walmart.

- *Melissa* received an immediate, tangible benefit in the form of a useful product sample and coupon.

- *P&G* gained more than it might have by blindly passing out samples on a street corner. By virtue of the Facebook Like, the company gained access to not just the person *liking* its page but to that person's entire social graph—information that P&G can now use to more effectively target promotions. Melissa's friends can immediately see what she's just liked and, potentially, go visit Walmart themselves and get their own sample, thereby giving P&G access to yet another social graph. Talk about the network effect!

- *Walmart* got more foot traffic in stores because of all the activity and social buzz around the vending machine. This, combined with the coupon on the back of the packaging, could equate to higher sales at that location.

- *The vending machine sellers and operators*, instead of just providing a piece of electromechanical dispensing machinery, can now tout that they are providing innovative new ways for brands to interact with their customers and prospects.

- *The wireless carrier* sells another data plan. Every carrier in the world today is interested selling data plans, and they are thrilled when they can do so on devices other than smartphones. A vending machine (and by association, kiosks, digital signs, etc.) represents a whole new category of device to support and capitalize on.

That's a lot of beneficiaries from one simple idea and interaction. It's especially impressive when you consider that it all sprang from combining two distinct, previously separate and unrelated worlds—the online social network and the stationary vending machine, the digital and the physical. It's a combination you will see much more of in the coming years.

If this sounds entirely too futuristic to you, consider this. The whole concept of *social machines* is simply an extension of the social contract most of us have already made with a powerful electronic device we carry every day—our mobile phones. If you are like most people, you could not imagine your life without it. Our lives have been inalterably changed by the absorption of this communications technology. It is so engrained that it has become virtually invisible. In fact, the Finnish have coined the term *kanny*, which roughly translates into "extension of the hand," to describe not only their mobile phones but their implied relationship with them. Like the watch on your wrist, its use has been completely enmeshed in your daily life. But make no mistake; it is indeed a *machine*. And it represents just the tip of the iceberg. Companies like Nike, with their successful Nike+ product line that combines fitness metrics with social networking, are unmistakable harbingers of what is to come.

As we will see, human cultures have been building relationships with machines for millennia. Stanford professor Clifford Nass recently conducted research that shows that it's not uncommon for us to attach very human qualities to our personal computers (which may explain the emotional reaction you feel when it crashes on you![1]). And although it is not this book's goal to delve deeply into cognitive science, it's worth noting that the whole concept of social machines as logical next step in the evolution of our relationship with technology is, in fact, supported by scholarship. Professor Andy Clark notes in his book *Natural Born Cyborgs*, "what is special about human brains, and what best explains the distinctive features of human intelligence, is precisely their ability to enter into deep and complex relationships with nonbiological constructs, props and aids." In other words, machines can teach us many things. We just need to include them in the discussion.

The obvious question arises: Is this just another uber-geeky concept that sounds cool on paper but fails in real life? The short answer is *no*—and the following are some good examples of why the concept stands a very strong chance of succeeding. Imagine a world in which:

- Your car shares valuable geographic, operational, and/or safety data with its "friends"—in this case, the other cars that are "following" it on Twitter—resulting in better gas mileage, ride-sharing opportunities, faster travel times, and the ability to find open parking spaces.

- Your house communicates with its occupants and other Facebook "friend houses" to share heating and cooling information, security data, utility usage metrics, and environmental measurements, resulting in improved energy efficiency and healthier, more secure homes and neighborhoods.

- Communities of elderly people securely and privately share health information that originates from various monitoring devices with one another, their caregivers, and their loved ones, resulting in lower medical bills, fewer hospital visits, better quality of life, and longer lives.

---

[1]http://www.cfo.com/article.cfm/6820151

- Retailers are willing to monetize your presence in their stores via discounts and promotions in exchange for the location data and/or purchase history on your smartphone.

- Literally hundreds of applications, services, and products that could be developed to capitalize on and support all the benefits listed here—which is just a brief snapshot of the potential areas for innovation. The social framework provides a completely new way of entering markets, demonstrating value, and driving adoption.

The best part is that none of these examples are fantasies. They are all possible today. The technology necessary to make them real exists and is getting cheaper every year. But ironically, the framework for understanding how we can harness these technologies has nothing to do with technology at all. The path forward for the utopian visions of home automation and smart cities is based on something far more mundane. It is a force that has driven countless revolutions before it: the inherent need we humans have to communicate, share our worlds, help one another, and improve our collective lot in life. In a word, this new universe of possibility is based on everything becoming *social*. As Clay Shirky mentions in his book *Cognitive Surplus*, "the use of social technology is much less determined by the tool itself; when we use a network, the most important asset we get is access to one another." We now must consider what it means to include machines in that mix.

As strange as it may sound, the concept of imbuing an inanimate machine with social characteristics is not only a logical, cultural stepping stone but it also makes sound *business* sense. The example at the start of this chapter is a real one, with real business value—and it's the first of many we will introduce in the coming pages. The fact is that by combining the best of what we've learned about sharing, collaborating, and cooperating via online social networks with everything we know about powerful, secure, potentially mobile, physical devices, we can create a stunningly rich new ecosystem for innovation. It is a new category for exploration that's part business and part consumer, maybe some hybrid beast called *M2C*—machine-to-consumer. Whatever acronym fits best, the concept rests firmly on the promise of breaking down the artificial barriers that exist between networked humans and machines.

After all, wouldn't we be happier with fewer mindlessly blinking DVRs, squawking car alarms, and inane error messages confusing the situation? Wouldn't it be better if we welcomed, instead of feared, the technology in our lives? Aren't there wonderful examples of big, successful businesses being built on making technology easier—the canonical example being Apple? To make this happen, we need to make machines a real, trusted, and more integrated part of our community, part of our *society*—which, coincidentally, leads us back to making things *social*.

To capture and discuss this new universe of possibility, we need a new dialectic that puts humans and machines on an equal social footing, insofar as it is related to improving the world and all those who inhabit it. That is the purpose of this book—to provide the framework, concepts, and vernacular to assist in the exploration and development of this exciting new world of communication.

CHAPTER 2

A Social Internet of Things

Social machines" is a framework for recontextualizing and reevaluating the business benefits of Internet-connected devices (the "Internet of Things") by integrating everything we've learned from social networks. It is a way to reframe the value of the Internet of Things to make it more approachable and meaningful to everyone, not just the world's geeks. This approach provides a new conceptual architecture for product developers that helps move the discussion from the purely hypothetical to the concrete—providing them a distinct and easy to understand point of view.

The social machines concept resulted directly from the client work my colleagues and I did at Bug Labs. We had been working to help our customers connect all kinds of things to the Internet—automobiles, postage kiosks, medical devices, vending machines, and stuffed animals . . . yes, stuffed animals (more on this later). All of this activity fell under the umbrella acronym M2M, which stands for machine-to-machine, a type of system that has been around for decades. In essence, this means that network-connected devices autonomously communicate with corporate data systems like inventory control, repair/ maintenance, accounting, or operations. The typical example is the photocopier machine that detects its toner is low or printing drum needs replacing and consequently "calls home" to an online service operations database and automatically schedules a maintenance call for the following day, all without any human intervention. This fantastic innovation has proved its value to businesses for many years. The return on investment (ROI) is based on driving down operational costs and improving the efficiency of service organizations. If a machine can communicate its status and eliminate the need for a field service representative to physically go and visit the machine, the savings would be substantial, especially for a large services organization.

But our customers were looking for something different, even though they could not put their finger on exactly what. And frankly, neither could we. We all believed—at least from a product development standpoint—that the Internet of Things was a trend worth considering. But was M2M and the Internet of Things the same thing? It didn't feel like it, even though technically they are very similar.

What we had to figure out was: How could we properly contextualize the value of something as frustratingly vague as the Internet of Things to customers? If this concept was so great, where were all the killer products? What was the Angry Birds of Internet of Things? Everyone had heard the promises of home automation, energy management, and telemedicine before, but the hype cycle on those notions expired years ago. We joked that all of these categories have been "about to be huge" our entire careers—much like artificial intelligence, another perennial favorite of the futurists. The M2M industry wasn't offering any help either and—to put it bluntly—its existing successes were pretty boring. I don't mean that in a condescending way. But only very specific areas of the commercial world get excited about fewer truck rolls, lower service inventory overhead, and higher asset productivity. We wanted to find a way to broaden its appeal without losing sight of the fact that it had to provide some kind of business value. So we plugged away and continued to try new ideas.

In retrospect, there were a few signposts that ultimately led us to this point. One, in particular, culminated in an aha! moment that became the seed for everything that came about very quickly thereafter—including this book.

Back in July 2009, I wrote a blog post for *Make* magazine (a publication that focuses on do it yourself [DIY] and do it with others [DIWO] projects) called "Hacking Health" (which can be found at http://blog.makezine.com/2009/07/08/peter-semmelhack-of-bug-labs-on-hac). It was based on my deeply held conviction that we would all live longer and healthier lives if we learned how to take better care of *each other*—and rely less on some giant, faceless, bureaucratic mother ship. The idea adhered to the same proven principles that open source software does—namely, community-based innovation, encouraging and empowering individuals to do new things without onerous overhead and administrative encumbrances (for example, licensing in the software world) and with an ethos of self-reliance. The reaction to the article was positive enough that I decided to put some of my ideas into action.

And, as are a lot of people who embark on such efforts, I was inspired by a topic close to home. My sister is a type 1 diabetic, meaning that she is depends on insulin injections to maintain a normal level of glucose/sugar in her blood. As she's gotten older, she's become susceptible to dangerously low blood sugar levels while sleeping. Normally, the human body would respond to such an event by turning on the adrenaline, quickly waking a person and prompting him or her to take action. But that was occurring less and less reliably with my sister. Thankfully, her husband and family took to watching out for her; however, that wasn't a foolproof system either. As we all became increasingly concerned, I scoured the market for some kind of electronic device that could help monitor this type of problem but was stunned to find that nothing was available. So I did what any other card-carrying geek would do. I decided to build one myself.

I give the full details of my experiment on my blog, so I won't go into it here. However, I will emphasize that the main point was to build a device that would issue online alerts/notifications and physically actuate things in my sister's environment (for example, turn on the lights) if she experienced a low blood sugar level. I immediately recognized I could neither safely nor comfortably directly monitor her blood (which would have required some type of ugly needle); therefore, I needed an alternative method of measurement.

Luckily, I discovered through conversations with doctors and diabeticians that there was a fairly reliable correlation between a low blood sugar level and a sudden spike in heart rate.

That was something I could monitor. So I combined a Polar heart strap, a BUGbase (a little, wireless, modular computer meant for hacking together new ideas like this—made by Bug Labs), and a power switch module to create a system that worked in the following way: At night, my sister would wear the Polar heart monitor and turn on the BUGbase on her nightstand. The strap would then send data wirelessly to the BUGbase as she slept. An application running on the BUGbase would then continuously track her heart rate. If there were a sudden, persistent jump in her heart's beats per minute, the device would immediately send out e-mail and text messages via its built-in Wi-Fi connection to a list of relevant individuals. And—here's my favorite part—it would turn on her clock radio at a blaringly high volume to wake up either her, her husband, or someone else in the house to come to her aid. It worked like a charm.

What happened next was just as interesting. The idea caught the attention of health information website WebMD, which prompted the question: What if online communities of diabetes sufferers could take advantage of this "hacking health" concept? What if they shared and pooled their information in such a way that others could evaluate and report on it? What if a content provider like WebMD could intelligently connect experts in the area—as well as relevant product companies—and expand the discussion that way? The possibilities exploded, and one of the things that became obvious through all this excitement was that it had *nothing* to do with technology. The core concept was simply the notion of *people taking care of people* and in some cases using technology to help. It was a sterling example of the power of a deeply interested social network looking for ways to improve their lives—where humans and machines were working together.

Jump forward a couple of years. This time it's not a medical device: it's a teddy bear. Let me explain.

There is a condition called chronic loneliness that affects more people in our always-on, constantly connected world than you might expect. The condition has a high concentration in the United States among the elderly, usually those living alone or in retirement communities. The reasons are fairly straightforward. We are probably all a little guilty of not calling or visiting our parents, grandparents, or elderly relatives enough. But sometimes what may feel like benign neglect can have far more serious consequences. People suffering from chronic loneliness can develop intense psychosomatic symptoms that end up requiring them to visit an emergency room, only to discover there's nothing physically wrong with them. They just *thought* they were having a heart attack. In reality—and heartbreakingly—they unconsciously just wanted to be among people who seemed like they cared.

A large health insurance customer of ours wanted to address this issue in an innovative new way. Based on research conducted by Intel in 2006,[1] they decided to create a new online messaging interface—aka, a teddy bear connected to the Internet—to let families communicate with one another via *hugs*. In this case, hugging one of these special teddy bears would in turn send the hug to another bear in the person's online community. The hug recipient's bear would then light up (via a little light on its chest), indicating that a hug was waiting. Picking up and squeezing that bear would result in a quick two-second vibration that translated into "hug given." It may sound dorky, but it was a huge success. It turns out that people respond very well to soft, cuddly, networked computers disguised as teddy bears. Although teenagers may take comfort in, and receive existential relief from, the SMS messages arriving on the cell phone curled up in the palm of their hand, most of the remaining population does not. In this case, Grandma demonstrated a measurably improved emotional state from interacting with the teddy bear that let her know that someone in her family wanted to give her a hug.

---

[1]http://www.intel-research.net/Publications/Seattle/100620061710_356.pdf

Now imagine integrating other types of health-related alerts and reminders into the bears' "vocabulary." Having a trusted, nonthreatening new friend in the house dramatically improves the chances of Grandma paying attention. Maybe she could be reminded (gently) to take her medications on time, to turn the stove off, or to call her doctor. Additional audio content could flow through the bear, thereby increasing its value and continuing to improve Grandma's health. Like the initial Walmart example in the book's introduction, this case demonstrates another win-win-win scenario. Grandma is happier, the insurance company's costs are lower, and the family feels closer.

Both of the examples discussed are similar in that each uses technology to improve someone's life—specifically, in terms of his or her health. The goal of the technology is clear: *to disappear*. If the application is successful, then the technology itself becomes invisible. The device becomes a friend, something to rely on, a capable partner. The diabetic heart rate monitor is a new health-monitoring buddy for my sister's family. The connected teddy bear is a source of companionship, connection, and affection for Grandma, artificial though it may be. These devices become enmeshed in the emotional fabric of their users' lives. They become *social*.

Last, we come to the aha! moment. As I stated in the first paragraph of this book, including an online social network in the mix of connected components created a state change in how I understood everything we'd worked on prior to that point. Suddenly, it became less about M2M and its technology-centric point of view and more about including machines as *peers* in a social graph. It became clear that everything we've learned about human interaction over a network—for example, via Facebook—could apply to specially developed devices on a network.

A critical aspect of this state change—and a key qualifier for all our customers—was its business value. Certainly, M2M applications make business sense. They are supported by a solid ROI based on operational savings and more efficient information flows. But whereas M2M has historically been about *saving* money, social machines revolve more strongly around *making* money. Or to put it in a less philistine way, social machines broaden the appeal of connected devices to a vastly larger audience. As such, its value to society is higher, its impact is greater, and its speed of adoption is much, much faster. This rapid pace of acceptance is one of the key strengths of the social machines concept. People "get it" and are eager to explore the benefits.

There's a reason ships have a gender (female). There're also solid reasons why we all love C-3PO and Thomas the Tank Engine and hate HAL. The human tendency is to categorize, whenever possible, new things into natural buckets with which we're comfortable—because doing so makes it easier to integrate them into our lives. Devices that don't get this treatment sit on shelves, blinking unhappily. The main addition I'm suggesting we consider is a sort of normalized form of network communication between those of us with hearts and those merely with hertz.

The great thing about a social machine is the interaction model. A now-famous caption from a 1993 *New Yorker* cartoon quipped, "On the Internet, no one knows you're a dog," which, if you're a machine, is an enormously liberating thing. You can now participate with humans in all kinds of ways that mimic human interaction. And what's more (and better), you can do an enormous amount more than any human could do. And therein lies the benefits of this approach. If we can successfully build, deploy, and include specially designed machines to participate in the social graphs of both business and personal networks in meaningful and relevant ways, we will have created a platform for real revolution. The examples I have referenced in this chapter are simply signal fires pointing the way to the much greater potential that awaits.

CHAPTER 3

Why Social Networks Must Evolve

Social networks must evolve because:
Everything will get connected.
Everything will get smarter.
Everything will get social.
We're running out of humans.

EVERYTHING WILL GET CONNECTED

According to the *Oxford English Dictionary*, a social network is "a network of social interactions and personal relationships." It's a definition thankfully devoid of technical nuance. Many people would be apt to think that social networks are a new and technology-centered phenomenon, given all the attention they've received over the past several years. But the concept and science of social networks have been with us for quite some time—way before Facebook, Twitter, and the countless other sites we've come to know and love/hate. Wherever there are humans, social connections form networks that, in turn, create what we call society.

Social networks are based on what we do best, or in some cases, worst: *interact with one another*. Every interaction in which we engage throughout our life has some impact on our network of family, friends, colleagues, enemies, and those we randomly encounter. Unless you're a hermit, the importance of these connections is self-evident. Interestingly, we interact and form personal relationships with lots of things—and only some of these are human. Pets are an obvious example of one of these non-human relationships. Those of us who have chosen to include animals in our lives can attest to their importance in our social graphs. People who have pets truly think of them as members of their family. Smart companies like Wag.com have actively tapped into this.

We anthropomorphize all kinds of things. Think about it: We give hurricanes and diseases human names. We also form *relationships* with *objects*. Ships have been named (and christened) for thousands of years, with aircraft being granted the same honors in the twentieth century. Cars have a long history of receiving this treatment as well. Just off the top of my head I can name Herbie the Love Bug (a Volkswagon Beetle from the 1968 Disney movie of the same name); KITT (a 1982 Pontiac Trans Am), which stands for Knight Industries Two Thousand, from the 1982 hit TV show *Knight Rider;* and, more recently, the Pixar movie *Cars,* a film in which every character in the film is a talking vehicle. Cars "run," have engines that "growl" and "purr," and have "sexy" curves and "intoxicating" power. Learning to drive is a rite of passage, attended by all the myths, legends, and lore that countless books and movies have drilled into our heads. I would argue that we exhibit this kind of behavior with cars because they have a symmetrical "face" that's similar to ours—two headlights for eyes, a hood ornament for a nose, and a grill for a mouth. We anthropomorphize objects in which we see ourselves or upon which we project our hopes, dreams, and imaginations.

The point is that we are wired to do this. By putting names on things and imbuing them with familiar qualities, we make them more approachable, more comfortable, and more lovable. We make them more human. As a designer, I can't think of a more laudable achievement than to create a product that people love so much that they accept it as part of human society, like the automobile. Not many have been granted that honor. In fact, many have been granted the exact opposite.

Take computers for example. As prevalent and critical as they are to our daily functioning, we all have a serious love/hate relationship with them. In the early 1990s, I had the opportunity to work in the computer services business. We dealt with many customers whose computers were not working properly. It was then that I came to realize that for most people, the most horrible thing, the most emotionally devastating event that could ever happen to them, absent a loved one dying, was having an un-backed-up hard drive crash. I have not witnessed since those days more rage, hysteria, and hopelessness. You would have thought that suicide was the only answer. It was that bad.

The personal computer seems like a vessel perfectly designed for limitless scorn. But, when working perfectly, it generates nary a compliment. There are few national clubs that lovingly care for, trade, and exchange old models. They never appreciate in value. They are wanted, even lusted after, for a millisecond in history, then forgotten almost immediately. For example, I have an original BlackBerry e-mail device, the iPhone of its day. I also have a PalmPilot. You want either? I also have a 1964 Corvette. You want that instead? I rest my case.

But why? These things should be our best friends. The trouble is in the interface. Personal computers today are still intimidating, technical mysteries to most people. Thankfully they are getting better, with companies such as Apple leading the way by vastly simplifying the interaction model. There are very good reasons why the iPhone has no menu bar, no windows, or multiple layers of pop-up dialog boxes. Simpler is better. But, for the most part, computers remain firmly rooted in the domain of the geeks.

Let's go back a little further in computer history and see what that can tell us about humans interacting with computers.

In 1950, Alan Turing, widely known as the father of computer science and artificial intelligence pioneer, devised the now famous Turing test as a way to determine whether machines could "think." More accurately, it was a test to see if a human could detect whether a machine or another human was answering questions submitted over a text-based network interface, like instant messaging. If the machine could trick the human into believing it was also human, it would pass the test. Hence, as far as the human was concerned, the machine was indeed thinking, at least insofar as anyone would think about answering the questions posed.

A key question that this test begs is, if you can't tell if the "person" you're conversing with over the network is human, do you care? Academically, I can certainly understand why it would be important, but from a practical standpoint it's immaterial. For example, if you ask the question, "Is there a long line at the Starbucks around the corner from me?" and the answer you receive is both quick and accurate, does it matter if the answer was generated by neurons or transistors? I think the answer is instructional. Why? Because Turing realized that for the test to work, he needed to create an abstraction. The network provided that service by creating a boundary between the two parties, one that denied the human participant the benefit of any sensory perception. The only interface was simple text in the form of a dialog. This, cunningly, let the human brain complete the abstraction—"I'm speaking with another human"—and form a connection.

The *New Yorker* quote at the start of this chapter captures the essence of this point perfectly—and it's famous for that exact reason. The Internet, or any network really, gives both people and (here's the important part) nonhumans (that is, things) *equal billing*. The network becomes more than a simple interface; it becomes a mask, an abstraction. On the Internet, it doesn't matter if you're a dog, a parrot, a child, an adult, a vending machine, or an automobile. If you can keep up your end of the dialog, then you're good. You belong.

Networked video gamers are used to this already. If you choose to make the computer your opponent when starting a game, for anything from chess to *Call of Duty*, you are, in essence, calling up a human stand-in—an "artificial intelligence," a machine—to play against you. In the most graphically advanced games, where the opponents actually look like human players, no one can tell who's real and who's fake. And it really doesn't matter. What's important is the experience and the challenge of playing the game. Your artificial opponent even shows up in the leader board, taunting you and your pathetic skills just like a real player. This is fascinating to me, because you endure the loss and enjoy the win just as intensely as if you were playing a human. The game is a truly social experience, despite the fact that you're the only human involved in it.

An *avatar* is the name the video game industry has given to a graphic version of ourselves in cyberspace. Originally a Hindu term for a deity who has assumed human form and descended to Earth, the term was initially popularized by Neal Stephenson's classic 1992 sci-fi novel *Snow Crash*. Later, the online game *Second Life* used what they also called avatars to allow you to *project* yourself into a three-dimensional graphical environment of stunning resolution and realism.

In games where you have human-like opponents, the software is presenting its own avatar. It's cloaking itself in a form that you understand and operating in ways that are familiar to you. But as we will learn, the computer can present an infinite number of avatars, only some of which are visual. Many will be audio only. Others will present themselves as tactile interfaces that vibrate or heat or cool. There are lots of interesting ways for computers to talk to you—and there are lots of ways for computers, and countless other machines, to be *social*. We will come back to the idea of a machine avatar later because it is a great way to understand the evolving interaction model I am proposing.

Last, I believe making machines more social, creating a more interactive and reliable societal bond, will vastly improve the human condition. A social machine is, in fact, a democratization of technology. It is a way of removing the arcane, opaque, and complex technical machine interfaces, decipherable to only the techno-literate minority among us and making information more freely accessible (for example, how many of you actually know that *USB* stands for universal serial bus, or for that matter, care?) I still vividly remember the first time I used Mosaic, Marc Andreessen's revolutionary new World Wide Web (WWW) interface called the Web browser. It radically simplified the navigation of all the information contained on the WWW. What used to require accurately assembling long, weird strings of words and characters into what was called a Universal Resource Locator, or URL (there was a time when "http://" was as good as

Swahili to just about everyone), was suddenly reduced to just a click of the mouse. I could instantly go from reading about some new Japanese painting in an online article to actually seeing a picture of it from an archive stored in a server in Tokyo just by clicking on a special underlined word or hyperlink. It was magical.

Gutenberg brought about a similar revolution with his printing press 300 years earlier. For centuries before, literacy was the exclusive domain of the elite few. Books were expensive, rare, and difficult to access. More important, all the information, knowledge, and wisdom contained in these books were unavailable to anyone but the nerds of that time—the highly trained *technologists* who could actually *read*. Gutenberg's invention brought the power of words and books to the masses. His presses enabled Martin Luther to distribute his heretical messages and launch the Reformation. Like Mosaic, the arrival of low-cost books— the democratization of literacy—connected more people to important information, and society flourished.

I'm not trying to suggest that the concept for social machines is on the order of books or browsers. What I am saying is that history has shown that when you lower the access barriers to information, wherever it's located, good things happen—humans find new ways to use that information to improve all kinds of things— science, medicine, culture, the arts. Information is rocket fuel for the human imagination. Right now there is an enormous pool of untapped information residing in all of the machines we've designed, built, and launched into the world. As I will show, gaining access to that information today is the domain of the ruling elite, the technical wizards we fondly call geeks. Collapsing those barriers and providing easy access to these untapped pools of data is the whole point of providing a new social interface layer. In many ways, you could equate the machines in our life as the unreadable books of centuries ago—and us the illiterate masses. Imagine the good we could all do if we had access to what is currently trapped behind unnecessarily technical interfaces. I argue that our imagination is the only limiting factor.

EVERYTHING WILL GET SMARTER

The other thing that's happening is the whole concept of what a computer is—and where computers belong in our daily lives—is rapidly changing. Nowhere is this more obvious than in automobiles. Even today's simplest models have up to 50 computers, in the form of microprocessors, running under their hoods or in their cabins. They manage everything from engine operation, to climate control, to antilock brakes and alarm systems. Many more advanced and luxury brands now boast actual desktop computer–grade CPUs that help run the communications, entertainment, and navigation systems. But even though your car is now becoming nothing more than a computer with wheels, your focus remains on its primary purpose—transportation, getting you and your family from point A to B quickly and safely. This is as it should be and is a great indicator of what's to come. Objects are getting smarter, becoming reliable partners.

But doesn't the term *smart* exaggerate what these computers can actually do? On one hand, yes, to the extent that *smart* means "intelligent," which implies actual thinking. But I find it interesting that we're starting to label products with advanced computing capabilities as smart because it is an indication of our willingness to ascribe to them descriptors normally associated with living things. Smart usually implies some sort of consciousness. Today, we're happy to call a computing device smart if it interacts with us in intelligent ways. A software program that makes us believe that it is actually thinking about stuff is a crowd-pleaser every time. Robots that motor around, respond to the environment, and talk to you produce the same reaction: smiles, laughs, and heads shaking in disbelief. It's almost as if we are eager to open our community to include these new "beings."

Smart, interactive machines that provide us with useful information, improve our lives, and generally make things easier will continue to make inroads in just about every walk of life. I think you'll find that there is a very short distance between a device being called smart and that same gizmo being labeled social. Which brings me to my last point . . .

EVERYTHING WILL GET SOCIAL

Recently, the *Economist* released its annual almanac of predictions called "The World in 2013." In an accompanying blog post, it highlighted the top 10 trends for business leaders to watch in 2013. The first one predicted:

> **Social everything: New generations and their digital world stepping forward**
>
> Social technologies are now a central part of everyday life and work. The social generations are reshaping companies from the inside, helping them to build broader, more agile networks to create and deliver value to customers. Mobility and connectedness will be at the heart of the future business environment: communications and marketing are moving from a focus on one-to-one relationships, to many-to-many.

I argue in this book that the definition and scope of social interactions and personal relationships will evolve to include inanimate objects of every kind—your toaster, TV, car, lawn mower, salt shaker—basically anything without a heartbeat—in the very near future. Although this may sound a little weird, it will appear normal in the coming decade. In fact, it's already happening with a fascinating mix of devices. Plants are tweeting when they need water. Health devices are posting metrics to your Facebook wall. Home security systems are texting you. Your smartphone is helping companies crowdsource traffic data. It's a seemingly futuristic idea that is moving into the here and now. Your social graph will grow to include whole new categories of *things*.

Wikipedia defines a *social graph* as "a sociogram, a graph that depicts [the] personal relations of internet users."* Notice how it doesn't say "personal relationships with or people"? Very prescient. Clearly, whoever wrote that definition knew that we would start developing relationships with things.

_____

*http://en.wikipedia.org/wiki/Sociogram.

My contention is based on two unstoppable trends. The first is our inexhaustible and accelerating desire to communicate faster and more clearly with one another and the world around us. For example, Twitter and Facebook are both leading the charge on redefining news reporting. It used to be good enough to just watch the 6 o'clock news or refresh your CNN Web page every hour. That's no longer adequate. People want real-time information from wherever the news is originating—instantly delivered via crowdsourced social media. The revolutionary Arab Spring has become the poster child for this new phenomenon. Another good example is that stock trading companies are now moving their data centers physically closer to the big exchanges (NYSE, NASDAQ, etc.) because the speed of light isn't fast enough for them anymore. In equity trading, execution is everything; every nanosecond counts. Therefore, the longer it takes for trading and pricing information to flow back and forth over a network between buyer and seller, the higher the chance of a lost trade. It is a life-and-death situation for traders. It matters so much that it's worth the multimillion dollar investment in new facilities.

The second is the inexorable pace of computer power, normally referred to as Moore's law. Briefly, this law states that computing power—as measured by the number of transistors manufacturers can squeeze onto a chip—doubles every two years. This basically means that every two years, you will have devices that are twice as fast but no more expensive. This translates into ever more advanced software and human-computer interfaces.

If you've ever used Apple's Siri product (an uncannily accurate voice recognition application that runs on the iPhone), you have an idea what I mean. This is why it's possible for the smartphone you carry to have more computing power than your desktop unit did two years ago. It's also why smart devices are starting to crop up everywhere. The cost of putting advanced CPUs into just about everything is becoming possible.

So, on one hand, you have humans reaching forward into the future, trying to interface more intimately and broadly with their world. And on the other, you have computers more and more capable of reaching back and interacting intelligently, either directly with us or over a network.

The whole concept of a social machine is defined by its active connectedness to the world—that is, its ability to interact in society, its ability to *share*. One could argue that this idea implies a certain social contract with the other members of the society within which it interacts, that machines, if indeed they are to succeed as social peers, also need some sort of "conscience" analog. This is not, in fact, a new concern. The author Isaac Asimov famously introduced his "Three Laws of Robotics" in 1942 that makes explicit this idea:

1. A robot may not injure a human being or, through inaction, allow a human being to come to harm.

2. A robot must obey the orders given to it by human beings, except where such orders would conflict with the First Law.

3. A robot must protect its own existence as long as such protection does not conflict with the First or Second Laws.

I love these laws because they demonstrate, in a very human way (rules, laws, obedience!), how we could reasonably live in harmony with our creations. If you believe the Old Testament, we're just following that example: laws! There will be many more discussions like this in the years ahead as we start to more closely embrace the machines in our lives. Truly social interactions require special choreography. Is it possible for a machine to have bad manners?

If you agree with my points, then it's impossible to not include the environment in the discussion—an issue that is a black eye for the electronics industry. In fact, I bet that today, Asimov would amend his laws to ensure that robots did not inflict any undue harm on Mother Nature as well. I see a social contract as a type of deal between the actors in a community (both living and inanimate), as they exist and operate *in their environment.* You can't view the community in isolation. And because there is currently no way to imbue a machine with any type of social conscience, it falls to the designer to build in the features necessary to help its users do the right thing. A truly well-designed social machine should include, in its makeup, an easy-to-understand and easy-to-execute method of returning its materials to a state where they can be reused, recycled, and/or reclaimed. In a growing number of countries, they call this cradle-to-cradle design (C2C), and it's a wonderful approach to this issue (for a complete rundown of this approach, read Michael Braungart and William McDonough's book of the same name).

You'll see in the next section exactly what I'm talking about, and strange as it may seem to you at first, I truly believe C2C will become the standard, de rigueur method of designing new physical things. Customers will demand a higher level of environmental responsibility from their product vendors and will reward those that demonstrate this sensitivity. The concept of social machines will enable a transparent, trackable, and truly auditable way of designing and building C2C-compliant products.

WE'RE RUNNING OUT OF HUMANS!

Let's examine Facebook. At last count, this de facto social network had over 1 *billion* users. That's nearly 14 percent of the world's population of 7 billion people. If we were being silly, we could conclude that if it continues to grow at its current rate of growth, it will run out of people with the computational capacity to access it in a couple years. Then what?! Does Mark Zuckerberg lie awake at night worrying that his company's growth will soon fall off a cliff? I have no idea. But I will say that his company's prospects improve noticeably by including all the machines in our world.

But forget Zuckerberg for a moment. It's much more exciting to look at this emerging trend from a different perspective—that of the product designer. What if you could tap into the wealth of social interaction data that Facebook provides to improve your products' quality, usability, value, and competitiveness, not only for the product maker, but for the users as well? What if you could build in features that made your products available for "social interactions," thereby making them part of the social network? Would that be useful? Absolutely—and in the next section, you'll find out why.

Let's go back to Zuckerberg now. It would not be hard to imagine Facebook embracing the notion of social interactions with nonhumans, as it would create a whole new playing field for value creation and business model innovation. Why would he want that? It's no secret that deriving profitable revenue from a hugely popular and free Web application via advertising—which is the chosen path at the moment—is tricky at best. Would adding social interactions with machines and other intelligent devices be a worthwhile direction to explore? Without question. And again, we will delve into this subject and see exactly how it works in later chapters.

The implied meaning of a social network must soon evolve and change. The concept of a social graph will expand to include many things that are important to you, not just the people in your life. As that happens, the value of all our social interactions will soar.

CHAPTER 4

Social Machines and the Future of Humankind

We live in a society exquisitely dependent on science and technology, in which hardly anyone knows anything about science and technology.
—*Carl Sagan*

Sybil rolled into Shinjuku late. Actually, it was early; around 2:00 AM. Everything had gone smoothly but nothing could prevent the raucous October weather that caused her flight delay. As she sat in the back of her cab crawling toward her hotel (this much traffic at 2:00 AM?), the fact that she knew exactly nothing about the latest happenings in Tokyo began to seep in. But she was used to the feeling—had gotten used to it over her past two years of ceaseless travel.

She came prepared. She unrolled her wireless computer screen and called up her Reality Graph, an application she had written last year that had made friends with every social machine in the city. Tokyo was much more advanced in this respect than most other cities and provided an unbelievable amount of data for anyone and everyone to see and use. The Japanese network carriers had managed to get virtually all product developers to put their products online, making available highly specific data sets from things such as parking meters, air conditioners, gas pumps, and taxicabs. In addition, private citizens, organized groups, universities, corporations, pirates, and criminals also published an unending kaleidoscope of data for others to build upon. The result was a bottomless pit of informational resources available for those who knew how to use it.

Sybil was one such person. From the moment she opened the Reality Graph, her social machine community welcomed her. She could use her Reality Graph dashboard to tell you everything—from where the cheapest diesel fuel was to the temperature of the water under the Rainbow Bridge. She could immediately discern which restaurants were the most crowded in her part of town (and what seating areas were warmest) and where to avoid buying cigarettes. She could review at a glance what stores were offering her the best deals on her favorite items, find a free parking spot, and see whether there was a line to check in at her hotel. The entire city—in all its dynamic, multi-faceted splendor—was, to her, nothing but a massive, glittering social network. And all she needed to do was access it. She had the app.

What happens to society when you start viewing connected devices as social peers on a network—when your daily life includes literal dialog with inanimate but smart social machines? If you consider Sybil from the vignette at the beginning of this chapter as an example, the societal benefits that come to mind for her revolve around words such as *transparency*, *accountability*, and *immediacy*. The society that Sybil inhabits is open to infor- mation flows that are impossible for us today. But I think their value is obvious. To better understand my point, compare this to a society based on secrets, the opposite of openness. Which world would you rather live in?

Right now, the machines in our lives can teach us many things. We just have to develop a framework for interaction. Or, put another way, I think it would be a great idea to call your car a friend. Some of us already do (for example, my wife calls her car "Luke"—as in Skywalker—it's a long story). And if you think your car makes sense, then why not other machines as well? Today we rely on a countless variety of machines to get us through our busy, twenty-first-century days. Our relationship with and reliance on these devices has already been firmly established. Whether you want to admit it or not, we have entrusted our lives to them. As a resident of New York City who lived through the devas- tation of Super Storm Sandy in October 2012, it is painfully— and mortally—obvious how reliant we have become. In this case, I think the best example is the electrical generator. Without these, there is no electricity—no lights, no appliances, no charging your cell phone, no transit systems. Without electricity, our modern society collapses. And in some places, it did just that. Violence, looting, hoarding, and other miserable human behaviors came to the fore, all because our high-tech machines failed us.

We are now, in author Bruce Sterling's words, a *technoculture*, a *technosociety*. In his wonderful book *Shaping Things*, published in 2005, Sterling discusses how cultures reach a technological tip- ping point, beyond which there is no turning back. He refers to it, dramatically, as the "Line of No Return."

"We know there has been a revolution in technoculture when that technoculture cannot voluntarily return to the previous technocultural condition. A sailor can become a farmer, but if the sailors from the machine era of iron and steam return to the earlier . . . era of wood and sail, millions will starve to death. The technosociety will collapse, so it's no longer an option. That's the Line of No Return."

I don't view this as a bad thing. I believe technology has improved our condition as a species and will continue to do so. I also see it as unavoidable. In many ways, it starts to feel like the process of evolution itself—just one that's going much faster. Humans and technology are inextricably linked. We are mammals with language and opposable thumbs; we are social toolmakers. We are a technosocial species.

Kevin Kelly, author of *What Technology Wants*, claims that "technology is an extension of life." And, like life, technology is on a trajectory of increasing complexity, variety, and specialization. The combination of life and technology results in an exponential increase in the speed at which the combination occurs. It's not difficult to see its path. Less than 15 years ago, we had no cell phones, no Internet, and no World Wide Web. Nowadays, it's nearly impossible to imagine our lives without them. Our societal, cultural, and perhaps biological evolution is becoming more tightly aligned with our technology evolution.

Therefore, if humans and their technology are coevolving, then it makes sense to focus that inevitability on something we could do well together—for example, sharing. Call it what you want, but at the end of the day, the core of *social* revolves around this fundamental concept. We simply need to enlarge the audience. And when we create social interactions with machines, we've just exploded the possibilities. As Tom Igoe suggests in his book *Making Things Talk*, talking is fine but gossip is where the real value lies because it implies the sharing of valuable, "juicy" information!

Obviously, the notion of literally making inanimate objects talk is a little unreasonable and, frankly, not entirely helpful. What I'm suggesting is making it easy for devices to communicate with us in meaningful ways using methods that we already use and value—speech being only one of these. The best way to make this happen is over a network of some kind because networks put distance between the physical and the digital. They allow the human imagination to work its magic and *pretend* that the thing on the other side of the connection is somehow sentient. Suspension of disbelief is all we need to make this work, because, whether the communicators are human or not, everything on a network is reduced to data—ones and zeros, electric pulses. It's "data democracy," and it makes enormous sense for the future of business for the following reason.

It has been said that "data is the new oil." One look at Google's market cap and founders' net worth and you'd be hard-pressed to disagree. Google deals in nothing but data, as does Facebook. Oil wealth is what propelled John D. Rockefeller to the pinnacle he still holds today: the richest man in history. There were plenty of other fortunes made from black gold as well. So if data is oil, it would seem safe to say that there are many more fortunes to be made using it.

However, there is another analogy I like to use as well—and it's one that helps frame the business discussion around social machines nicely. Data is the new *steel*. And for the record, Andrew Carnegie, founder of United States Steel Corporation, is the *second* richest man in history.

Why is steel a good metaphor? Data, like oil, *flows*—not through pipes but through wires and radio waves. But unlike oil, data itself can be built upon. Facebook, and I mean the entire company, was built on top of your data, my data, and that of a billion other individuals. And to further the example, the company Zynga—which provides free online games—was built on top of *that*! These companies have been built on humans' social network data. Twitter is yet another example of this; it is a company whose entire value is based on your data flows, specifically your tweets. That's it. Data was the steel needed to build these companies. And there are, and will continue to be, many others. Now imagine what we could build by using the data from both our own and our machines' social networks.

The point is simple: Stop thinking of machines as physical things and view them solely as sources of data. We need to see them as collections of information we can use to build new things—new products, customer experiences, and even whole companies. This is the future.

So where's this all going—and what does it mean *practically* to the product developer and businessperson? What will we find indispensable 15 or 50 years from now? Something tells me it will have technology at its core. And therein lies the Shangri-La for all future inventors, product developers, entrepreneurs, and tinkers of all kinds; what features/functions do your new products need to have to reach that pinnacle? I predict that the most important features you will add to your products in the coming years will have to do with *data*.

Indeed, what is the definition of a product at all when everything becomes interconnected data? For an example of what I'm talking about, Google search "3D printing." It's a type of technology that basically "prints" physical objects. There's lots of good information on the Web regarding how this actually works; however, from a product developer's standpoint, the concept is as disruptive as it is revolutionary. Let's say you need a special plastic part, for example, a cover or gear, to fix something at home. Today, you'd have to special order it from the manufacturer and have it shipped to you. Best case is you'd have the part the next day.

But in the future, that same manufacturer will just offer the 3D printing *data* necessary to "print" the gear whenever and wherever you need it. And it's not just capable of printing small stuff. You can print an entire product. Think about that for moment. That product you just designed won't be made in China. Someone in Des Moines or Timbuktu will print it. The complicated manufacturing process that normally accompanies the creation of physical products gets completely eliminated; there's simply no more need for an intermediary in this way. As a designer, you are responsible for only one thing—*data*.

A terrific example of this just appeared in one of my Twitter feeds this morning. Try to digest the monumental implications of the following headline:

Staples Will Offer On-Demand 3D Printing in Stores[1]

Today, we've already internalized that written documents are really just bits and bytes that we can render in physical form (aka print) anywhere there is a printer and a network connection (Figure 4.1).

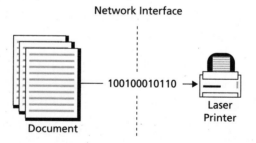

Figure 4.1   Laser Printers Convert Bits into Documents

It won't be long until we feel the same way about physical objects. Just because a product has three dimensions does not mean it is not still just a collection of data (Figure 4.2).

---

[1]See the Resources section for more information and the link to the press release.

Network Interface

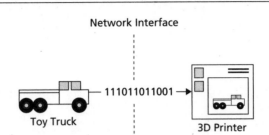

Figure 4.2   3D Printers Convert Bits into Physical Objects

POINT—A physical object is just data wrapped in hard edges.

With that context, it makes perfect sense that product design needs to evolve to meet these new challenges and capitalize on the commensurate opportunities. The discipline of design will start to recognize that once a product is "liberated" from its material form, interesting things can happen.

From a design perspective the most startling change this liberation causes is the realization that all products will now have *two interfaces*. The first is the tangible, physical interaction model we are all familiar with: the LCD screen, buttons, levers, displays, speakers, and other devices our five senses can engage. The second interface is the *digital* and is accessed over a network connection. This is the product's *digital avatar*, its presence, makeup, and profile on a network. Figure 4.3 presents what I mean. On the left-hand side you have the "real" product: a refrigerator. It has all the familiar physical properties you would associate with it. The right side is the product represented as pure data. It's a digital representation of the real product and has its own properties. Don't worry about what the terms mean; we'll get to that later. Just recognize that the design of social machines requires some new thinking.

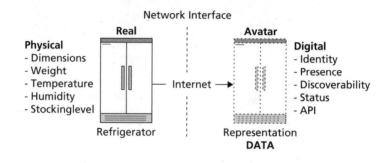

Figure 4.3   Social Machines Exist in Two States—Physical and Digital

The same user may access both interfaces, but often there will be a split. Similar to today, there will be the typical "end user" like you and me who, in the case of a refrigerator, uses it to keep food cool and as a place to stick an endless number of magnets. But there will also emerge a different class of users—developers—who will be more interested in the device's *avatar*, its data "exhaust" on the network, than in the product's physical interface. Today we take for granted that our smartphones run applications. But that was not always the case. Ten years ago, cell phone designers were not concerned at all with third parties accessing their hardware over the network. It just wasn't part of their product vision. Fast-forward to 2012; there isn't a designer in the world who isn't interested in developers.

I contend that there will—and should—be developer interest in virtually every product that's put on a network. But this interest depends entirely on successful avatar design. Designing avatars will become critical if the goal is to attract the best and brightest developers. How this new digital interface appears to developers, what data are offered or aren't and to whom, and what control it does or does not bequeath on the developer and, in turn, his or her end users will be what makes or breaks a product in the future. Apple has done a superb job of this, and the results speak for themselves.

Tomorrow's successful product designers will understand that their creations can never again exist in isolation. They will need to survive on a network. They must switch effortlessly between serving end users and developers equally well. They will need to deeply internalize that their products are nothing but *data*. But with this challenge comes an unprecedented opportunity to radically alter the very definition of what a product is, as well as the value that it can provide to the world.

Pip Coburn, author of the book *The Change Function*, argues that people today feel "naked without data." That is, we have become so used to having a universe of information in our pocket/purse/bag in the form of a mobile phone that when we are without it, we feel vulnerable, unprepared, or even disrobed. The fascinating thing about this is that the idea makes sense only if you think about it terms of online data. In reality, you're surrounded by information and data 24/7; you have been since you were born. It's information made available through your five senses (and sometimes your sixth—that sense of intuition we all have and that's especially strong in mothers). But for some reason, that type of data is boring to a lot of people—at least for the moment. On the other hand, the data available via LinkedIn, Twitter, or Yelp is far more interesting (for now). Elevating social machines to the level of social peers can and will change this; these social machines will become both conduit and catalyst.

I'm probably guilty of overstating my case in this chapter's title. However, I am convinced that our collective future will be intimately intertwined with the concepts I've laid out here. The rest of this book explains how to start bringing some of these ideas into practice—so that we can all begin to benefit from the results.

PART II

Every Product Is a Platform

Rethinking Product Design in the Age of Connectedness

A designer is an emerging synthesis of artist, inventor, mechanic, objective economist and evolutionary strategist.
—*R. Buckminster Fuller*

CHAPTER 5

Overview

I decided to write this book because I became convinced that there is a sea change coming that will have an enormous impact on just about every aspect our lives. It is a deeply positive change that will allow us to live happier and healthier. It will help us make better decisions. We will use natural resources more efficiently and take care of Mother Nature in the process. It will help us build better businesses that more accurately address the real needs of people everywhere. All this will happen because we will start to get much smarter about interacting with all the physical objects in our daily lives. We will develop products that don't sit in isolation but live on networks, with us. As Sean Parker's character in the movie *The Social Network* famously said, "First we lived in villages, then we lived in cities, and now we are going to live on the Internet." Guess what? We won't be alone there. Billions of machines will be joining the community too, and our world will improve because our information will improve.

Let me give you one simple reason why: feedback loops. Both humans and machines use them to rapidly coordinate with one another and improve whatever task is being undertaken—driving a car, flying a plane, or controlling the temperature of a house. In the June 2011 issue of *Wired* magazine, author Thomas Goetz describes them well:

> "The basic premise is simple. Provide people with information about their actions in real time (or something close to it), then give them an opportunity to change those actions, pushing them toward better behaviors. Action, information, reaction. It's the operating principle behind a home thermostat, which fires the furnace to maintain a specific temperature, or the consumption display in a Toyota Prius, which tends to turn drivers into so-called hypermilers trying to wring every last mile from the gas tank. But the simplicity of feedback loops is deceptive. They are in fact powerful tools that

can help people change bad behavior patterns, even those that seem intractable. Just as important, they can be used to encourage good habits, turning progress itself into a reward. In other words, feedback loops change human behavior. And thanks to an explosion of new technology, the opportunity to put them into action in nearly every part of our lives is quickly becoming a reality."

Social machines can help us all improve. The rest of Part II is devoted to articulating, as best I can, how I see that process unfolding and what I believe the steps will be to participate.

CHAPTER 6

A Brief History of Abstraction

The advent of social machines is ensured simply because it is in our nature. It is an unavoidable progression whose roots go back thousands of years. It's based entirely on our deeply ingrained ability, desire, and need for abstraction.

If there is one thing all my research found as I hunted for a logical and historically supportable foundation on which to base all my arguments it was this: We are a species of abstractors. We would all still be living in caves (if we survived at all) had we not mastered the power of abstraction. It is generally agreed that the reason *Homo sapiens* rule the world today, whereas our evolutionary brethren—Neanderthals and *Homo erectus*—died out, is because we developed language. It allowed us to use symbols (sounds → words) as stand-ins for real things. The following illustrations show how this basic starting point has put us on an unstoppable path toward a future populated by social machines (and beyond).

Language gave us the ability to convey facts, ideas, and concepts to others without them having to actually experience the reality themselves. Take, for example, the concept of temperature. We can all sense hot and cold. But without language, the only way for me to convey to you how cold it is outside would be to drag to you out into it. I suppose I could make motions and expressions that gave you the sense of it, but for you to really understand what I was trying to get across, there was only one

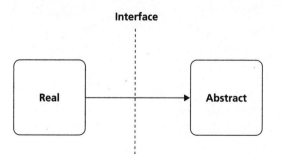

Figure 6.1   Interfaces Provide Opportunities for Abstraction

path: experience it yourself firsthand. But with language I am able to abstract the reality of a freezing cold day into a bunch of logically sequenced sounds that I can make using my mouth. And because you recognize those same sounds as words, you can experience what I have without actually experiencing it yourself. You need to force yourself to imagine an existence without this basic ability to even come close to understanding its power. If you've ever read the book *Miracle Worker* by Helen Keller, you get a great sense of the massive cognitive transformation language provides.

The abstraction of real-world experiences into a logical sequence of orally produced sounds slowly inspired the desire to record those sequences in ways that could be repeated by others. We wanted the ability to store knowledge, to enhance both our personal and collective memories. We realized that by building a storehouse of communal knowledge we became a stronger and wiser community. Spoken words were abstracted into symbols that could be written or drawn onto some material external to ourselves, and hopefully more permanent and resilient. The

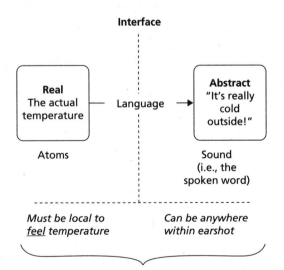

Figure 6.2   Words as Interface

power of this abstraction, the written word, was equally powerful to human advancement. Collections of written material became books, which became book collections and then libraries. I don't need to spend any time explaining the influence all of that had on human history. The fact that you're even reading this is testimony to that![1]

The next major phase of our species' march toward greater and greater abstraction was converting the symbols scribed on pages into special codes that could be transmitted over long distances. Sure, books are a great storehouse of information, but you need to have the book in your possession to access its contents. What if you wanted to share a funny passage in a novel with a friend a thousand yards away? Well, you'd have to go over to your friend or have such a loud voice that you could shout to him or her.

The French invented the telegraph, which, for the first time, gave us the ability to share words over long distances quickly. Starting out as elaborate machines that displayed graphic symbols that could be spied with a telescope from another station (say, a mile away), it quickly evolved into electric pulses over copper wire and into what we now know as Morse code. The telegraph, it has been argued, was more transformative in its day than the Internet has been for us. Because, for the first time ever, we were able to abstract a physical artifact—a spoken and/ or written word—into a series of codes that could be transmitted instantly over long distances and decoded into its original form. It is hard to grasp the impact this new abstraction had on the world. In Tom Standage's book *The Victorian Internet*, he claims that the telegraph, or the "highway of thought" as it was called (remember the information superhighway?), "unleashed the

------

[1] I recognize that I'm leaving out a whole area of human achievement that would also have been impossible without abstraction—mathematics—but I felt it was sufficiently like the written word to not divert too much more time to it. In fact, one could write a whole book on the history of abstraction, not something I'm trying to accomplish here. Hence the title "A Brief History . . ."!

greatest revolution in communications since the development of the printing press." It's an apt analogy for this timeline. Both inventions introduced a new category of abstraction, and human advancement accelerated at a torrid pace.

The telephone followed on the heels of this success, but although it was a revolutionary advance in its own right, the world had already been monumentally changed. Distance had been collapsed. Voice was just icing on the cake.

The telegraph also paved the way for what came next—the further simplification and abstraction of those electrical impulses into what we now call binary code, or the language of digital computers. Based on the physical behavior of a vacuum tube (that is, until the transistor replaced it) to maintain one of two states—on or off—computer engineers were able to reduce just about everything into a series of on-off sequences represented by 0 for off and 1 for on. You've probably seen binary written as a mysterious sequence of ones and zeros since it has become the hallmark of all things geek. My name, for example, in binary is 10101110 11101100 01001000 11101100 11011000. Catchy, isn't it?

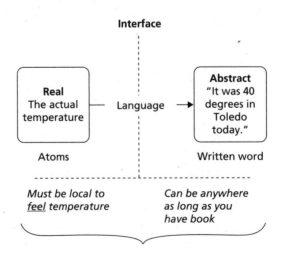

Figure 6.3   Books as Interface

This binary language/abstraction formed the basis of all things digital and propelled yet another revolution in human thought and advancement. What used to take 100,000 physical pages of paper and ink could be now be stored on an electrical device the size of a paperback book. What once would have taken a ridiculously long and complicated series of manual mathematical steps on paper could now be done in a matter of seconds. Problems whose solutions seemed out of reach just a few years prior were suddenly approachable. Again, I don't think I need to waste your time justifying the importance of digital computing on our society and the world at large. It is virtually immeasurable.

It quickly became apparent to the computer engineers of the world that one computer working in isolation was powerful, but many computers working together was more powerful still. Like the telegraph had shown a hundred years earlier, sharing information radically increased its value. So computer networks were born to allow computers to emulate their human designers: to share information, cooperatively address tasks, and generally get things done faster and more efficiently.

The early networks were slow, clunky, fragile, and vulnerable. But they accomplished their intended mission (at great cost). In fact, ARPANET, the world's first working packet switching network and father of what we now call the Internet, was born in these early stages. Initially, only expensive mainframe computers were connected to networks, but that quickly changed with the invention of a new, much lower cost "personal" computer architecture. The microcomputer revolution of the 1970s gave birth to a host of new network technologies and approaches, the most important of which was Ethernet. This technology now forms the basis of everything we do on the Internet.

The Internet, like all networks, provided a new abstraction layer. Users were oblivious to the geographical location of the computers with which they were communicating. Whereas before you needed to travel to where the computer was operating,

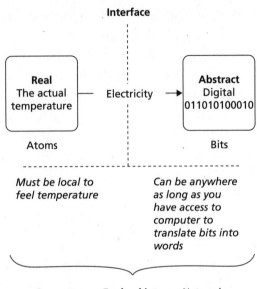

Figure 6.4   Bits as Interface

with a network connection, the computer, in effect, came to you. It didn't matter if it was located in Boston or Buenos Aires; you accessed it the same way. The information stored on physical devices located all over the world were now available from your desktop (wherever that was). All you needed was an Internet connection.

Which brings me to the last illustration in this brief, incomplete history of abstraction. What are networks evolving into now? I will argue that in many ways networks (and by that, I mean *networks of computers*), and the incredibly advanced technologies that enable them, are starting to accomplish what may be the hardest task of all. They are becoming *ubiquitous*. And in the process, they are becoming invisible. Networks are now so enmeshed in our daily lives that we don't even notice them anymore. They are becoming part of *society* itself. There is a quote that I like from David Weinberger's book *Too Big to Know* that seems entirely appropriate here (emphasis is mine):

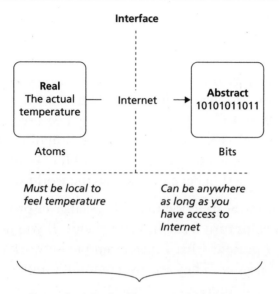

Figure 6.5   Network as Interface

As knowledge becomes networked, the smartest person in the room isn't the person standing at the front lecturing us, and isn't the collective wisdom of those in the room. The smartest person in the room *is the room itself*; the network that joins the people and ideas in the room, and connects to those outside of it. It's not that the network is becoming a conscious super-brain. Rather, knowledge is becoming inextricable from—literally unthinkable without—the network that enables it. Our task is to learn how to build smart rooms—that is, how to build networks that make us smarter, especially since, when done badly, networks can make us distressingly stupider.

What I like about this quote is the value he places on the network, not as a simple communications conduit but as an explicit part of the design. Networks are foundations on which we build value chains. The most famous to date is the World

Wide Web. You cannot talk about the Internet without including it. From this foundation, all that we know of as social has sprung. A social network *is* the Web to most users. It is on top of *this* framework that we must now build. You already know what I call this next phase. I make a distinction between what's now called a social network and social machines only because the definition for the prior is always based on human communities. But in reality, my definition of a social network combines both humans and machines because I believe that is how the world will evolve.

What is the abstraction that the social layer provides? Social abstraction helps turn facts into knowledge. If you take a look at Figure 6.6, I present what I mean. Simple network connections have no social value. They are just communication channels. But by adding social filters and parameters, you start to add value to the connection because you provide context. You may be able to collect gigabytes of data from the world's Internet-connected computers, but turning that data in valuable information is hard. Social abstraction makes it easier by providing the context you need to filter, analyze, and qualify raw data.

For example, there was a time when people would look for jobs and post their candidacy in the Classifieds section of the newspaper. The Internet gave us Craigslist, which drastically

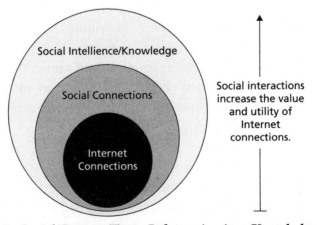

Figure 6.6   Social Context Turns Information into Knowledge

reduced the costs for and improved the visibility of both job seekers and hirers. But today we have LinkedIn, which not only gives both parties a place to post their information, but layers on a deep, rich set of social network features that allows people to learn vastly more about either the job candidate or job poster. LinkedIn turns basic job-related data into valuable, timely, and actionable information and knowledge. There is literally no comparison between the initial Internet-enabled job boards and the social network–powered sites like LinkedIn. The social abstraction brings tremendous value. One look at the market cap of LinkedIn and you will need no further convincing. And like every other abstraction phase that has come before, a whole new set of opportunities and challenges awaits those who want to build upon it. Just ask Zynga, the company that literally built itself on top of Facebook and went public based on the success of their approach. It is a perfect example of what I presented earlier. Data, when combined with the power of social context, is the new steel. There are many more Zyngas out there.

So, why did I bother to present all this history? Because with everything new comes the inevitable eyebrow raising. I wanted to lay a solid factual foundation for what I really want to declare—a manifesto of the type that probably wouldn't have gone over too well right at the start of this chapter but may make more sense now.

There needs to be a shift in how product designers and developers view their jobs. It is no longer good enough to build the perfect widget—a gloriously beautiful artifact that would look fabulous in the Museum of Modern Art. More than 100 years ago, the Industrial Revolution forced a dramatic change in product development. Mass-market production demanded special approaches, techniques, and designs. As valuable as all that has been, we need to enhance it. Going forward, a successful product will not be defined by unit sales alone. Indeed, what good is that metric if users actually manufacture their own products in their basements using their three-dimensional printers?

Success will be determined by how well your product works with others, how *social* it is. It will be defined by how much revenue *others* derive from its use, how many others use it as scaffolding for their own success. True, long-term, culturally important products will be those that become foundation stones—steel—for others to build upon. Apple's success has many facets, but I would argue, its most important is that it has built, nurtured, supported, and grown a worldwide ecosystem of other companies and individuals that use its products to achieve its own success.

This is the true power of this new phase of abstraction. Social products will be successful based on their value to society—the community in which they operate. Isolated, stand-alone products will feel like desert islands. They will seem archaic and slightly vain. Social machines will interact with one another and their users in valuable new ways and unleash a new wave of innovation.

CHAPTER 7

Social Product Design

People don't want gadgets anymore.
They want services.
They want services that improve over time.
—*Jeff Bezos, Founder, CEO,*
Amazon.com, Amazon Kindle Press
Conference, September 6, 2012

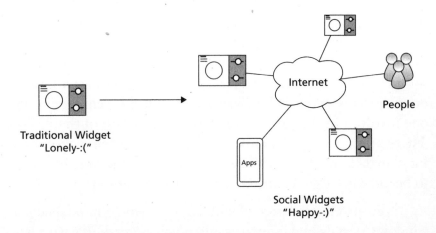

Figure 7.1 The Best New Products Will All Be Connected *and* Social

Gadgets as we know them are dead. Companies building unconnected hardware products will face unrelenting market pressures from those that do, forcing them to compete on the least desirable attribute: price. When you buy an unconnected product, you are buying a quickly depreciating asset, whereas a connected version could actually appreciate in value over time. A disconnected product is obsolete almost immediately. A connected product stays fresh by participating in online communities comprised of digital content sources and other devices (see Figure 7.1). Connected products offer the opportunity for continual customer interaction and potentially new revenue streams. A disconnected product is a dead end. You sell it once, and you, the seller, have received all the economic value from it that you ever will.

Conversely, companies that put connectivity at the core of their products' capabilities will discover significant new green fields for innovation. At the 2013 Consumer Electronics Show in Las Vegas, this concept emerged as one of the primary themes of the show. Forbes declared 2013 the "break-out year for the

Internet of Things."[1] A huge variety of connected products were demonstrated, eclipsing 2012, in which more than 50 percent of the products on display were Internet-connected. There will soon come a day when the vast majority of the devices introduced are connected. Why? Because it just makes sense for everyone involved in the production and consumption of the device. There are too many benefits for all parties. It even makes sense for planet Earth. The longer you use a device, the longer it takes to become garbage. Connectivity is a green feature.

New products, designed with connectivity in mind, become windows, portals, and interfaces into much larger digital worlds—content, communities, and social interaction. If you look at the design of the Amazon Kindle, physically examine it, you'll see that it is a case study in minimalism. It's an LCD screen in a plastic box with a couple of buttons. You'd be forgiven for thinking it was a tray of some kind. But turn it on, connect it to a network, and it becomes a looking glass through which any number of adventures can begin. It is an elegant physical interface to a virtually limitless digital world. It is the forerunner of a much larger revolution about to begin. Connect anything to a network and it instantly becomes more valuable—to both the customer and the maker. The network gives the product life, with the data available via that connection its blood flow. Connected products are dynamic and vital, not isolated and diminished.

CONNECTED VERSUS SOCIAL

As wonderful as connectivity is, it turns out there is a big difference between being *connected* and being *social*. Ten years ago, we all had e-mail addresses on the network. Today, more than one billion of us have a social graph on Facebook. Kids don't even

---

[1]http://www.forbes.com/sites/ericsavitz/2013/01/14/ces-2013-the-break-out-year-for-the-internet-of-things

use e-mail anymore because it's *not social.* The world is awash in networked computers, phones, and other gadgets. But right now, *none* of them are social. Ten years from now, we'll be scratching our heads wondering how we could have lived like that.

The term *social* implies *more than one.* For example, a community is social; a hermit is not. Today, virtually every product is a hermit, sharing nothing with anyone. A *social* product design places the idea of community at its core. Its design accounts for the fact that it will exist in a world of multiples—customer types, user interfaces, usage scenarios, and other networked devices with which it must coexist and communicate—potentially billions of them! And, like humans, communities of social devices are stronger, more resilient, and more useful than single, isolated gadgets. Hence, it is worth designing them.

But creating a social machine implies much more than just sticking a network connection in a product. A January 2013, *BusinessWeek* article puts it succinctly, "There are plenty of connected devices out in the market . . . But the key to building out a true Internet of Things experience isn't in being able to connect devices to the Web, but building a service based around that connectivity."[2] We often see this with our own customers at Bug Labs. Once the network connection is in place and working, the very next question is always, "Now what?" The natural starting point for answering is by asking another question: "Who's the customer?"

You may recall that in Part I, I mentioned that a new class of users—*developers*—would need to factor into designers' plans. In fact, there are three distinct social machine customer types that need consideration. You have the primary, classical customer; the person who actually buys the physical product. You also have the second class of customer, the *developers*, who will be attracted to

[2]http://www.businessweek.com/articles/2013-01-03/ces-2013-connected-devices-and-the-internet-of-things

your product based on the services it offers over a network connection (its *avatar*). Last, you have the customers of the *developers'* output—the *developers' customers*, who are the buyers of their applications that utilize the social machine in some way. The needs of all three customer types are very important for social machine design.

For clarity, I will refer to them throughout the rest of the book as follows:

- Primary customers—the actual purchasers of the social machine/device

- Developers—the customers for the device avatar

- Developers' customers—the customers for the developers' products and applications

In addition to the expansion of the customer definition, what are some other things a designer needs to consider? Let's review a few of the concepts I've introduced so far.

1. Network interfaces are abstractions that free physical objects (people included) from the bounds of location and provide the opportunity for them to communicate with others.

2. A social machine takes advantage of the fact that networks are good for creating illusions. They let us play make-believe. Remember the quote "On the Internet, no one knows you're a dog."

3. Social machines are defined by the *data* they produce and consume over a network.

4. Social machines communicate via digital entities called avatars. These avatars need to be *designed*. As weird as it sounds, this concept will help as you try to determine your product's "identity" on a network.

And this brings us to Jeff Bezos's quote at the beginning of this chapter. People don't want gadgets; they want services. They want a product experience that improves over time. But isn't the Kindle a gadget? If you use the standard definition for a gadget, then yes, it is. But Bezos introduces the Kindle differently. To him it's a network interface, a window, into the vast, growing Amazon content catalog. The Kindle is less a thing and more a portal. For Bezos, it is about data, and the Kindle's design reflects this. The Kindle is data wrapped in plastic.

This makes a huge amount of sense for everyone. Amazon establishes a mechanism through which it can continue to sell you its products. Customers benefit by receiving a product that defies obsolescence and delivers additional and useful value over time. Content creators benefit because they receive a new form of distribution. And finally, the environment benefits because the product's life span increases dramatically, thereby keeping it out of the landfill. It's a win-win-win-win.

But is the Kindle social? Fortunately, the answer is yes—it is a great example of an early social machine in action. Why? Because it places the notion of community at its core and uses its network connection to do more than just upload and download content. It uses its connection to engage, share, and participate with others. For example, the Kindle allows you to share your reading status, book ratings, text highlights, and notes. These are all social features that the designers needed to keep in mind when developing the device. We'll discuss the hows and whys of this in much more detail later in this chapter.

The Kindle also uses its connection to engage with the critical *second* type of customer: developers. Amazon has provided what I believe is the most crucial element for all social machines: a development environment. This allows third parties to add value and extend the usefulness of the physical device over time and absolves Amazon of having to come up with all the great ideas themselves. Keep in mind, Steve Jobs did not invent the game Angry Birds. The Kindle is not only useful for customers, but it's a platform for developers.

Let's return to Bezos's assertion that customers want services and analyze what he means.

A *service* is defined as a product you experience over time, like a taxi ride or a movie. Amazon's primary *product* has always been a service: *delivery*. Amazon has never written the books or recorded the music CDs, but it has delivered them reliably and consistently. Kindle *services* are a continuation of that basic product. But unlike the physical delivery of real objects, digital deliveries can imbue products with a special quality: the ability to improve over time. That means the Kindle you have today will be even more valuable tomorrow, and the next day, because you will continue to download new content. A library with a thousand books is more valuable and useful than one with a hundred. As Amazon continues to offer compelling new content for delivery, Kindle customers will benefit. Their Kindles will "improve."

This basic equation underlies the explosion of interest in finding ways to offer services to customers via physical devices such as the Kindle. Today, you can select from a growing catalog of devices that partake of all these content delivery services—smartphones, tablets, laptops. They all seek to use services to improve their value to customers.

In some respects, Amazon has it easy. We have all been trained how to consume and work with digital content. We all know how social networking works. The Kindle, which is really just a handheld computer, capitalizes on this familiarity. So when the original Kindle designers sat down to think about what they needed to include in their innovative new e-book reader, the customer usage model was fairly well defined and proven.

But what if your company is not Amazon? What if your organization neither creates nor delivers digital content? What if there is no well-established usage model to piggyback on? If social machines are truly a new way to envision product design, then shouldn't it apply to all products, not just the "easy" ones? The answer is an emphatic "yes," and I will attempt to show you how it applies in the following sections, where we'll look at a wall-mounted weather station, a wheelchair, a hand sanitizer dispenser, and a bicycle. I think you'd agree that none of these appear easy!

EXAMPLE 1—THE WEATHER STATION

We've discussed that a social machine is much more than just a device with a network connection. To demonstrate what I'm talking about, I'll use a simple product as an example: a wall-mounted weather station. This familiar device is great for displaying, usually on an LCD screen, the local weather conditions based on atmospheric sensors enclosed in the device or located nearby, connected either wirelessly or via a cable of some sort to the main unit. The weather station also contains a low-power microcontroller (a simple computer) to manage the process of organizing the sensor data and presenting it properly on the graphical display.

As we discussed earlier in the section on abstraction, for users to benefit from this disconnected computer, they need to actually be within viewing distance of it. To read the display, you have to be able to see it. So, unless you have a remotely accessible webcam pointing at its display screen, you need to be in the same room as the weather station to use it as it was designed. Nothing wrong with this approach, but if you believe Bezos, this type of product is a dinosaur. It is DOA.

But let's see what happens when you give the same device the ability to communicate on a network, specifically the Internet. We won't change anything else but that (Figure 7.2).

The easiest way to grasp the benefits of this new capability is to envision a Web browser accessing the device's data and displaying it on a Web page. For the sake of simplicity, we will skip

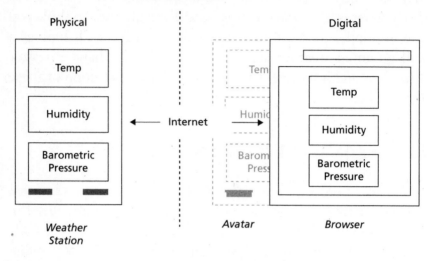

Figure 7.2   Network Interface Frees Information from the Physical Device

the avatar interaction, but you can see it in the illustration. We'll come back to it later. As I mentioned earlier, a network is good for abstracting location. So a Web connection to the weather station makes it possible to access the local sensor data from anywhere on the planet—as long as you have access to the Internet. The Web browser becomes the new user interface displaying the data coming from the physical weather station. In essence, you could view this as the weather station providing a weather data *service* to the browser that is accessing it.

But that's just the beginning.

Once the data are freed from the confines of the physical device and made available on the Internet, you are free to share that information with others on the network. This is the basis of a social machine. Like the Kindle's ability to share your reading activities, the weather station can now share its own data. As you might expect, these data have a variety of interesting uses above and beyond just being viewed remotely via a Web browser. The data can be used as input for applications that run outside the device. This is an important new capability. The weather station is built using a simple microprocessor, which does not have the capacity to run complex applications itself. But you can imagine lots of applications that *could* be written that would make great use of the data being produced. The apps would just have to run somewhere other than the weather station, a trick we will discuss later. But for now let's just look at some example applications.

Dashboards

- Interactive graphs and charts showing weather data trends over time

- Query and search of historical data

Notifications and Alarms

- Applications that send e-mails and/or SMS messages when certain conditions are met or thresholds exceeded

- Timers that periodically send updates to your Facebook wall

- Twitter updates based on specific conditions

Analytics

- Applications that provide statistical information based on the data provided, mashed up with other relevant, Internet-based data, for example, traffic data, air quality data, calendar data

Health and Wellness

- Remote monitoring of the interior conditions of an apartment or house to determine whether any health or wellness risks are being experienced by the occupants, both humans and pets

Crowdsourced

- Submission of data from weather station users to a collective pool to thereby create a real-time, distributed, weather-sensing framework composed of a highly granular set of individual contributors

All of these options become available by viewing the isolated weather station with a social machine lens. By adding a network interface layer to the weather station, you elevate the product beyond mere gadget status. You can add services to the product experience. You can continually upgrade them, improve them, and enrich them. You can offer them for free, charge a fee, or both. You can make the services available via a browser or dedicated application. Finally, you can make it available via desktop, mobile device/smartphone, or kiosk. Creating a way for customers to interact with the product in new and valuable ways helps you create a dynamic and ongoing dialog with them. This not only helps you compete but helps you build a better product.

Another important thing happens when you empower the weather station with network communications capabilities. As I mentioned earlier, a weather station's microcontroller brain does not normally have enough computing power to run applications on its own. However, the network connection solves that problem by allowing the application logic to run on a computer located elsewhere while consuming the weather station's data— its *weather data service*—over that connection (see Figure 7.3).

There are two common approaches. The first arrangement is sometimes called cloud computing because the actual computer running the application is seen as running in the network cloud—that is, somewhere else on the Internet (the actual location is immaterial; remember, networks abstract location). With this architecture, the application can, whenever it's required, access the weather data service over the network as if the sensors were local to it. As a product designer, this is liberating because you can avoid the time and cost required to enable your device

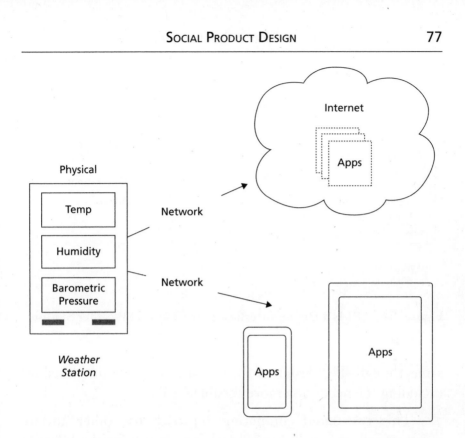

Figure 7.3 Network Interface Allows Application to Get Written in the Cloud or on other net-connected devices

to run applications itself, which would normally mean including a more complex and expensive processor/CPU. By pushing that capability into the cloud, you vastly simplify your product. And better yet, you can include application functions and capabilities that would have been impossible to offer otherwise.

The second approach involves running the application logic on an individual's smartphone. Like the cloud computing approach, the application accesses the weather data service over a network as required. But unlike the cloud solution, the smartphone doesn't necessarily have to use the Internet to connect to the weather station. The network connection could just as easily be established via Wi-Fi or Bluetooth, both commonly available options on most smartphones today. The effect is the

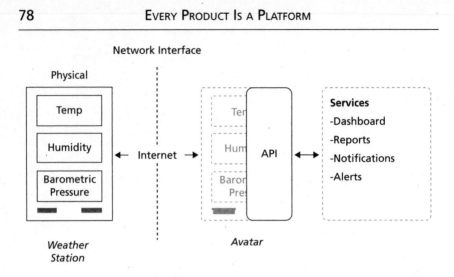

Figure 7.4 API Is a Digital Interface to the Physical Weather Station

same, though. The design of the weather station is simplified by excluding the need for a more capable CPU.

This two-tiered computing approach has other advantages as well, especially if the goal is to maximize the benefits of a social machine design. If you choose, you can make your *application architecture* available to others, meaning you make it easy for third parties to access the weather data service you've designed into the device. The most popular way to do this is via a something called an API, or application programming interface (see Figure 7.4). This is a well-documented set of rules or methods for interacting with the device over a network connection. Amazon's Kindle has a very well-defined API, as do all of Apple's products.

On one hand, the idea of exposing your product's data to the public may feel like you're inviting disaster, but the benefits far outweigh the costs. Sharing data allows third parties (aka software developers, see Figure 7.5) to write applications that address diverse customer needs and/or solve real business problems. By opening up this capability, you leverage the power of worldwide developer communities to explore new ideas and

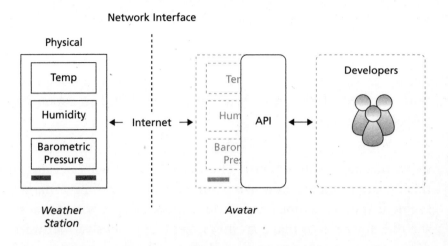

Figure 7.5   Developers Use API to Build Applications

uses for the device. Although this direction is by no means a sure thing—just because you throw a party doesn't mean everyone (or anyone!) will come—it is another example of the power of social machines.

The health and wellness example I introduced earlier provides a good example. It would probably not be the case that a weather station manufacturer would target the health care market segment. But by designing it as a social machine, the manufacturer can leverage the expertise and interest of someone (or some organization) that does. Let's say that there is a particular group that helps parents with children who suffer from juvenile asthma. This is a small target market that would have difficulty supporting the big investment necessary to build a new, dedicated device. One could never achieve the scale required to reach a consumer-friendly price point. But an off-the-shelf *social* weather station with an open, cloud-based development environment could provide exactly what's necessary. In this case, let's say there is a high correlation between high humidity and the onset of certain asthmatic symptoms. An entrepreneur could offer a kit that sells the weather station and access to her new cloud-based application that monitors it for high and/or rapidly changing humidity levels and alerts a preset group of individuals—parents, care givers, friends, and so on. All the developer needed to do was write the application; no need to raise investment capital or build an expensive custom device.

This is a perfect example of the type of win-win-win scenario social machines can achieve. The device maker wins because a third party is adding new value and driving sales into a market segment they were not focused on. The developer wins because she did not have to make an investment in expensive hardware design, testing, and production. And clearly, the customer (and the market in general) wins because it's now possible to get access to an innovative and useful new product that directly addresses a need that most often is ignored entirely because the economics of investing in it did not work.

You can literally take this example and apply it to hundreds, if not thousands, of products you currently know and use. Every product can benefit from this type of network connectivity in many of the same ways we've discussed.

EXAMPLE 2—WHEELCHAIRS AND HAND SANITIZERS

Let's talk about wheelchairs and hand sanitizers. These are probably not items that spring to mind when thinking about the possibilities of social products, but bear with me. This real-world example is illustrative of how unique problems get solved when you connect previously isolated devices to the Internet.

Problem statement: Hospitals incur significant costs via wheelchair "shrinkage." That is, hospitals are losing track of these expensive assets over time. And when it comes to counting inventory at the end of each month/quarter, they are discovering they don't have as many as they should. No one wants to say they're getting stolen . . . so . . . it's called shrinkage.

Wheelchair   Hand Sanitizer

Figure 7.6   Wheelchair and Sanitizer

Wheelchair designs are traditionally a purely mechanical affair, with the main goal being to provide a flexible, safe, and reliable platform for transporting people in a sitting or reclined position. As such, their basic structure has not changed much over the past few decades. Of course, there are the more advanced motorized versions of the wheelchair, but these are not the standard issue provided at hospitals due to cost, complexity, maintenance, and so on. There is also very little incentive to make them anything other than mechanical devices due to the aforementioned shrinkage problem.

There are lots of clever, high-tech ways to keep track of objects as they travel around. It's easy to assume that the now ubiquitous GPS technologies would be the best answer for the wheelchair. However, even though there are many advantages to GPS, it would not be a good solution here. The main issue would be that GPS signals don't work well indoors, because most GPS receivers are not sensitive enough to pick up the very weak satellite transmissions that GPS needs. But the more pernicious issue is far simpler and presents an obstacle to just about every technical solution that comes to mind: power. Most of the approaches to tracking things revolve around radios of some sort, and they all require power, sometimes lots of it, to operate properly. But we just said in the prior paragraph that normal wheelchairs are mechanical vehicles, and adding cost in the form of high-tech electronics would be counter to prevailing wisdom on wheelchair design. Installing batteries, CPUs, and radios onto a standard wheelchair doesn't make sense.

Let's switch now and talk about hand sanitizers—not the normal plastic bottles you buy in the supermarket nor the fancier wall-mounted versions you see everywhere these days. The ones I'm talking about are the hospital grade dispensers that sit on a stand and get heavy duty workouts every day—for good reason. Hospitals are becoming increasingly vigilant when it comes to the spread of germs. As a result, they are installing automated hand sanitizer dispensers that are activated by a hospital employee's ID card. The goal is twofold. First, it ensures hospital staff are keeping their hands clean by visiting a dispenser a certain minimum number of times each day. Second, it improves the health of patients by introducing them to fewer germs and other pathogens. Easily generated reports show who is in compliance. Because the doctors, nurses, and other medical staff need to use the dispensers frequently, they are installed in many convenient locations, never more than few steps away. Often, these devices are attached to the hospital network so that information technology (IT) staff can run hospital-wide reports with just a few clicks of the mouse.

What do hand sanitizers have to do with tracking wheelchairs? Let's think about it from the standpoint of social product design. A product is nothing but data. In this case, the piece of data we're most interested in is the wheelchair's location. Given the constraints that we know of already—no expensive electronics allowed—how can we determine the whereabouts of the wheelchair? This is where the hand sanitizers come in. As we saw in the preceding paragraph, a large number of dispensers normally get installed throughout the hospital. Because these dispensers don't usually move, their location is known. The service these dispensers offer is *communication*.

So if we could find a way to pair up wheelchairs with whatever dispenser is closest to it, we would be able to determine, roughly, where that wheelchair was. And as the wheelchair moved through the hospital, you could keep track of it. You could even watch its movement in real time if you so desired. But what would we use to do the pairing? Didn't we already rule out the idea of any technology that needs power? Yes, but it turns out there is a way to do this in a way that requires no power-hungry circuitry. It's a technology called RFID (radio-frequency identification), and it's changing the way objects get tracked. In essence, it's a special type of product tag that contains very unique information about the product to which it is attached. When the tag is blasted with radio waves from a compatible transmitter, special electrical components in the tag vibrate in response. This uniquely identifiable vibration creates a return radio signal that can be detected and decoded by the nearby base station or RFID *reader*.

If we put RFID tags on all the wheelchairs and equip each dispenser with an RFID reader (another nice thing about the dispensers is they are always near wall outlets), we've come very close to solving our problem. By using the built-in network connection on the dispensers, we can access the RFID information and feed it to an application running in the cloud. The dispensers become very much like the weather stations in the prior example—network nodes sensing local conditions and sharing them with others. And similar to that example, applications can get written in the cloud that continue to add value to the solution. It can continue to evolve and improve.

With this passive tracking system now in place, you can use it to keep track of all kinds of things—basically anything to which you can adhere a tag. The opportunities are fun to think about. And the more you do, the more you recognize their real value.

How is it social? It's not hard to envision using a system like this to keep track of not only the wheelchairs but the people in them. Hospitals could track not only the wheelchairs' location but their status: empty or occupied. Patients could be given incentives for returning wheelchairs to specific locations—for example, using Foursquare for check-ins. Tweets could be sent if a wheelchair exited the building and systems updated when certain waypoints were reached or thresholds exceeded. Patients could use the system to look after one another. Information could be shared and new value created. Many possibilities exist.

EXAMPLE 3—THE SOCIAL BICYCLE

Assignment: You've been asked by a major global bicycle manufacturer to design the bike of the future. This kind of request either thrills or terrifies designers (maybe a bit of both). It's a chance to make an enduring mark on an industry, but it is also an incredibly tall, scary order. With bicycles it's especially difficult because their design has essentially remained unchanged much of the past 150 years. Yes, materials have made huge advances, but in the end, it's still two wheels, a seat, pedals, and handlebar. It's a beautifully simple design where adding to it actually diminishes it. But by viewing the challenge from a radically different perspective, you'll see there is an enormous amount of innovation still available.

The key to unlocking the possibilities is to consider the three types of customers I introduced earlier and think about the bike from the perspective of each. If we break it down, it looks like this (see Figure 7.7).

There is always the chance that all three types are the same person—a passionate rider who develops and consumes his or

Customer type	Interested in . . .	Product
Primary customer	The bike itself—the physical specifications, characteristics, and qualities	The physical bicycle
Developer	The bike's avatar—the bike's static and dynamic (operating) information provided over a network connection	The bicycle API and development environment
Developers' customer	Using an application to benefit either an individual biker or community of riders	The application

Figure 7.7   Three Customer Types

her own applications—but in general you can consider them separate.

The primary customer will buy the bike for all the traditional reasons: low cost, fun and healthy transportation, great form of exercise, and so on. The developer, on the other hand, cares about one thing: *data*. The developer will want to consume the *services* the bike offers over a network connection. The best way to envision the needs of the developer is to see the bike from the network's perspective. With that lens in place, the bike becomes nothing but a collection of data sets that, if designed correctly, becomes available for others to use to do cool things.

To jump-start your imagination, here's a listing of some (not all) of the data sets one could obtain from a network-connected social bicycle:

Static Data

- Physical dimensions—literally its size, weight, proportions, etc.

- Bill of materials—what parts, from what manufacturer, have gone into making this specific bicycle

- Manufacturing data—who manufactured the bike, when, and where

- Recycling info—what parts are available for recycling and how to do it

Dynamic Data

- Operating data—wheel RPMs, pedal RPM, pedal orientation (right and left), pedal force (right and left), gears in use, braking activity (front and rear), frame orientation, vibration, acceleration, tire pressure and temp (front and rear), riding weight, front fork orientation, drivetrain configuration, seat height, orientation and temp, handlebar height and orientation, date, time of day

- Environmental data—ambient temp, relative humidity (RH), barometric pressure (BP), air quality, light level, wind speed/direction, UV level

- Geospatial data—compass heading, latitude/longitude, altitude, inclination, rate of climb/descent

- Network data—connection type, signal strength, account status, modem status, network ID

- Bike frame information—temperature, stress, flex

- Hub fastener tightness

Application-Level Data

- Security, identity, presence, status (see next section)

- Battery status

- Version history

- Diagnostics—hardware, operating system, software

- Maintenance information

If you let your imagination wander as you look at these data sets, I think you will start to recognize the types of applications that could get written. Keep in mind that the apps may be useful not only for individual riders but also for groups, organizations, manufacturers, and so on. The point is, once a bike is abstracted into a collection of data points, your design ideas are freed from the constraints of the physical world. Better yet, as the designer of a social machine, you are not responsible for figuring out the killer app. Believe it or not, this comes as a surprise to most designers because it's natural to try to figure out a great use case for all your design handiwork. But the reality is, the best ideas almost always come from unexpected places.

As I mentioned earlier, one of my favorite examples of this is the fact that *Steve Jobs did not invent Angry Birds*. That was the brainchild of some guys in Helsinki, Finland. I'm relatively certain that when the iPhone was being pitched to the Apple Board of Directors, there was no mention of a game involving birds, pigs, and slingshots. But what Jobs did create was the most attractive platform (both technically and economically) for luring in the best and brightest game developers. As a result, Angry Birds is probably responsible for driving a decent volume of iPhone sales just by itself (which actually doesn't even matter since Apple takes 30 percent of all Angry Bird application sales; another beautiful thing about its model). As an aside, Apple has an interesting track record in this regard. Back in the 1970s, the Apple II was just another microcomputer competing for business (and neither the largest nor most successful). That was until a guy named Dan Bricklin decided to develop Visicalc, the world's first spreadsheet application on his own Apple II. The success of this application, all by itself, drove Apple sales through the roof and helped position Apple as a business tool and more than a mere hobbyist's gadget. It was the first software killer app, selling more than 700,000 copies in six years—on 5.25-inch floppy disks!

The point of focusing on your product's data attributes, in addition to its more traditional feature set, is simply this: You never know when the next Dan Bricklin will use your product as the basis for the next mega-success.

Let's consider some application ideas using the data sets from the preceding list. Forget for the moment *how* these data become available to a developer (we'll cover that in the next section). I think you'll be pleasantly surprised by all the possibilities.

Individual Rider

Fitness

- Combine operating, spatial, and environmental data to provide a comprehensive view of not only the performance of the bike and its rider but how the environment is affecting that performance. Pair this data with a personal health monitor (heart rate, blood pressure, etc.), and you get a complete picture of how riding a bike, and in what capacity, helps optimize the rider's fitness.

Maintenance

- Log operating and environmental data to build reports on usage. Application could set thresholds and notifications to perform routine maintenance based on normal wear-and-tear, but could also alert the rider to potentially dangerous mechanical conditions if a specific component is not replaced or action performed.

Safety

- Using the spatial data (location information), the application could remotely keep track of a specific bicycle, positioning its location on an interactive map (à la Google Maps). This would be good for parents trying to understand the whereabouts of their children in the neighborhood.

- Logging operating, environmental, and spatial data could provide the ultimate "black box" for riders, insurance companies, police, physicians, and so on, providing extensive details about the state of the bike just prior to and/or during an accident.

Efficiency/Green

- By logging and analyzing operating, spatial, and environmental data over time, a report could be generated that allowed riders to see when and where they are riding most efficiently.

- Applications that access the manufacturing, bill of materials (BOM), and recycling information stored in a bike could make it easier to do the right thing when it comes time to get rid of a bicycle.

Entertainment

- Bike performance data could easily be stored and analyzed, providing a way to compare today's performance to prior records. It could also be used to run comparisons with others on the network. Game dynamics could be used to encourage riders to push themselves to higher levels of performance and fitness. Others could comment, praise, and insult their performance if it were posted online.

Groups of Riders

Racing Clubs

- Bikes that publish their performance data in real time would provide racing clubs with the basis for all kinds of applications that could make tracking racers easier and more fun. Riders and race viewers could access up-to-the-second race information about individual riders or teams.

Gyms

- Gyms and fitness centers could write applications that help members keep track of past performance and encourage new achievements. Members could elect to share their data and set up competitions. Gyms could use these apps and data as a competitive weapon to attract new members.

Friends and Family

- In the same way that keeping track of an individual biker could help parents' stress levels, so too is it useful to have the ability to track multiple bikes simultaneously and in real time.

Organizations

Rentals

- Rental bike companies operate with small margins, so applications that help them keep their inventory in use and good repair would be hugely valuable. Applications that help track where riders go could help companies optimize rental locations, offer targeted promotions, better understand usage patterns, and so forth.

Repair Shops

- Bikes that publish their diagnostic information could provide bicycle repair shops what automobile repair facilities have had for decades—a quick, reliable, and effective way to get to the root of a problem quickly (with cars, huge amounts of operational data are available via a special port under the steering wheel, called an OBD-II port). Operating history and usage logs could also provide a wealth of useful data that would make repairing a bicycle faster and more effective.

Retailers

- A bike that works with applications would be a retailer's dream. Not only could it provide a competitive advantage (aka higher margins) over retailers offering only disconnected bikes, it could provide a mechanism for the retailer to continue the dialog with customers over time in the form of application updates, new apps that may be of interest, new data sets that could be useful, or all of these. Connecting the bicycle to the Internet opens up entire new avenues for innovation for retailers.

Physicians/Physical Therapists

- Riding a bike is a great form of physical exercise, but most of us don't do it properly. In many cases the bike is not adjusted properly for how we ride. Or how we are riding is not efficient or, worse, is doing us harm. Applications that keep track of not just performance data but things such as seat and handlebar adjustments, pedal configuration, and force while pedaling would help doctors and physical therapists design and monitor programs that help riders get the most out of every ride.

Journalists/Media

- Imagine a magazine review of new bike that included not just commentary on the normal stuff but the quality of its data! A bike's rating would begin to move inexorably toward connectedness as a key value driver. Journalists and the media could use this access to verify manufacturer's claims and, conversely, publish their own.

Health Insurance Companies

- Imagine an application that put dollars in your bank account if you hit certain performance targets or that lowered your premium if you maintained a specific record of activity over time. It would be a no-brainer win-win for both insurance companies and riders.

International Associations

- Large associations such as the Olympics would welcome a standardized way to access the performance data coming directly from a network-connected bicycle. They could offer applications that viewers could download to watch and analyze racers' performance in real time and match it to historical statistics.

Government

Traffic/Congestion Control

- Cities have a vested interest in decreasing the volume of cars and trucks on their streets. By developing applications that make bike riding more appealing, they can help achieve their goals. It's not hard to imagine cities offering tax incentives for net-connected bicycles that could use the applications written by them and, in some cases, help crowdsource useful, real-time information about the city itself.

Green Initiatives and Incentives

- Bikes don't pollute, and they help riders get healthier/ stay healthy. Both of these things help cities reduce costs. Applications that help cities achieve these ends would be extremely valuable.

Safety

- Cities are dangerous places for bikers. Applications that help riders pinpoint where accidents happen most frequently or demonstrate what conditions are likely to increase the chance of an accident (maybe even in a certain area) would be a welcome addition to most rider's smartphones. Connected bicycles would make obtaining this data easy.

Manufacturers

Usage Data

- It's not hard to imagine scenarios whereby a manufacturer offers a discount to riders willing to share usage and operational data with them. Applications that anonymize and package reports for manufacturers' use could be a great way to achieve this. Manufacturers benefit by obtaining the Holy Grail of data sets from their users—actual information about the use of their product. Customers benefit from lower prices.

Warranty Data

- A bike that can verify when it was manufactured, verify what parts are original, and provide key operational data could help manufacturers and authorized warranty repair shops to do a better job of providing this important service.

This is not an exhaustive list. There are many additional applications that could be written, especially as you start to consider specific use cases and vertical applications. I'm sure a bike rider in India would have some amazing ideas that I would never dream up.

The other key aspect that bears repeating is, once a bike becomes a network node, it breaks from the path of guaranteed obsolescence. The customer experience of the bicycle can now improve over time, its usefulness extended and enhanced in marvelous new ways. Communities of bikers can group together and share data in much the same way that Waze (waze.com) is doing for automobiles and driving. New businesses can be built that help improve the availability and safety of bicycles. The list goes on.

What have we learned by examining these three very different product types? Doing these types of exercises helps develop a new way of thinking. It helps designers realize and remember that they are now responsible for satisfying the needs of a larger collection of customers. You will most likely have the needs and requirements of your primary customers in hand. You can use all the traditional tools in your tool chest to get smart(er) about those. But what about that class of customer I'm calling developers? How do you gauge their needs, their interests, and their requirements? How do you make sure you provide the features and functions *they* will need to satisfy *their* customers, the developer's customers? Although this is all new and unexplored, I think there are some fundamental attributes that form the cornerstones for all successful social machines.

- *More is better.* If you have the option of exposing/sharing more or less of your product's features online, err on the side of *more.*

- *Open beats closed.* Offer open APIs and open source libraries for connecting to your product.

- *Documentation is as important as the applications.* Nothing speaks louder to new developers than clear, well-written documentation on how to use the API. It adds immeasurably to the developer's experience of the product.

- *Provide incentives to share.* Everyone benefits when people share their data and/or applications. So provide incentives to developers to share code or data from their apps. Companies like GitHub (github.com) do a great job of this with their pricing. If you agree to keep your code out in the open, you can store it there for free. If you want to keep it private, you pay. You can also offer social rewards such as posting badges or broadcasting tweets or dispensing with other social capital to encourage sharing. Do this correctly, and the benefits will flow not only to the developers but to the developer's customers, too.

- *Never stand still.* With a traditional product, you design it, you build it, and you sell it. Done. This is not true with a social machine. The sale of the device is the beginning, not the end, of the dialog with your customers (all three classes!). As such, you will be judged by all three and praised/pilloried publicly based on how well you manage those dialogs. Social machine design is dynamic. Velocity is a strategic competitive weapon. If your customers think you're asleep at the wheel, not innovating fast enough, offering new value, or listening to their needs, they will find a new vendor that does. Get ready to respond!

To understand the design "essence" of a social machine, you should unlearn a couple of things you know about products and relearn one very important skill (something you did naturally as a child). You need to restart seeing things as they *are*, not merely as they're supposed to be. As you 'll see in this part, in product design there are the features you actively include, but there are also what I 'll call tacit features that come along for the ride and, for the most part, are ignored: by you, the designer, and the user/ customer. You need to expand your design sense to not only recognize these qualities but to actively seek and take advantage of them during your design phases. I consider these new qualities the *social* feature set. Here's one of my favorite stories that nicely illustrates the point:

When I was still developing our initial product for Bug Labs, I had the opportunity to sit down with my then seven-year-old son and four of his friends. I painted the following picture for them. "I just bought a doghouse for my dog, Vader. It's a nice doghouse, I think. But I'm not sure he feels the same way. Obviously, I can't just go ask him! So I'd like to find a way to see how much he uses his new doghouse. The problem is, it's placed in the backyard in an area I can't easily see it from the house. I don't want to sit out there and watch, because that may influence his behavior. Nor do I want to set up a video camera that would record hours of video, because then I'd need to sit there and review *hours* of video! I want you all to be product designers and come up with a new gizmo that will help me answer this simple question: How often is Max using the doghouse? At this point I put a bunch of LEGO bricks on the table, each one labeled with a different function:

- Motion detector
- Camera
- Air sniffer
- Wireless communicator
- Thermometer
- Light sensor

I then asked:

"If I could build a gadget to help me figure out how often Max was using the doghouse, how could I use these different blocks to help?" After some explanation of each brick they came up the following ideas:

- "Max stinks, so the air sniffer would tell you when he was in the doghouse and when he wasn't!"

- "If Max was in the doghouse, the temperature inside would go up and we could measure that! Then use the wireless communicator to text you what it was!"

- "We could hook up the motion detector, the camera, and the wireless communicator so that it would take a picture whenever it sensed motion and send you an e-mail!"

At no point were they ever concerned with *how* this would get built. Every "service" was just a LEGO brick. They weren't at all worried about the fact that some sensors may be USB-based, while others might have a standard serial interface. They were thinking purely functionally. They were intuitively seeing the sensors as service providers, for example, the motion detector "speaking up" if it saw any movement or the thermometer broadcasting its readings.

From a social machines perspective the implications of this are interesting. In this case, the different modules providing the "services" were all from one company, but that does not have to be the case. In the future, the services from all types of social products will be available for mixing and matching, like LEGO bricks, and not just by seven year olds. Developers will come to expect that social machines all have tacit features available for exploration. Consumers will recognize and more highly value products that support this type of thinking. The key point is, product developers will need to anticipate this activity and account for it in their designs. They will need to see their products from the point of view of the network—what functions and services will they provide? Social machines need to work well on their own, but more important, must play well with others.

CHAPTER 8

Avatars and the Social Seven

Unique Characteristics of Social Machines

W hen designing physical products, we concern ourselves with all the familiar issues that define, restrict, and organize our world. All physical objects have the same basic properties. They have dimensions—length, width, and height. They have weight and mass. They have important other properties such as color, texture, proportion, and even smell. We are intimately familiar with all these qualities because they make up the world we live in.

But what happens when you connect that product to the Internet? If all it will do is download data from the Web or some other Internet-connected server, then none of the social concepts we've discussed thus far will be of much use. On the other hand, if the goal is to truly design a social machine, then how your product appears on the network is important.

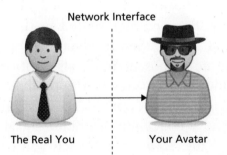

Figure 8.1 Network Interface Introduces New Attributes

Your product's network "appearance" is what we've been referring to as an avatar. It is exactly similar to the avatars we use in current networked environments of humans. But instead of creating a digital representation of a person, we're creating one for a machine. As the designer, how you do this will influence how well your product performs its social functions.

Referring back to our social bicycle example and considering both our primary customers and developers, the diagram shown in Figure 8.2 can be drawn.

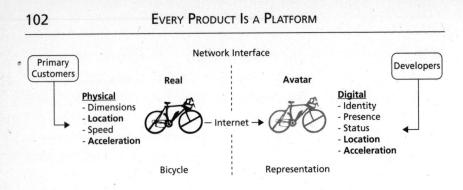

Figure 8.2   An Avatar Is the Developer's View of the Real Product

Similar to how people decide what "features" they want to expose in their own online avatar, social product designers also get to determine what product qualities—aka data—will get revealed on the network. In Figure 8.2 you can see that two pieces of information are represented in the avatar: location and acceleration. The other product data sets—dimensions and speed—are not exposed. You'll also notice that there are a couple of additional features in the product avatar that are not part of the physical bicycle: identity, presence, and status. These are part of a collection of unique social machine attributes that I call the *social seven*. Which you choose to use or ignore is entirely up to you and is driven in large part by the target customer/market.

The Social Seven—Overview

The whole point of connecting a device to a network is because you want to facilitate communication. You want the ability to exchange and share information with other devices on that same network. But establishing a network connection is just the beginning. To take full advantage of what a network connection can offer, social machine product designers need to consider the key attributes illustrated in Figure 8.3.

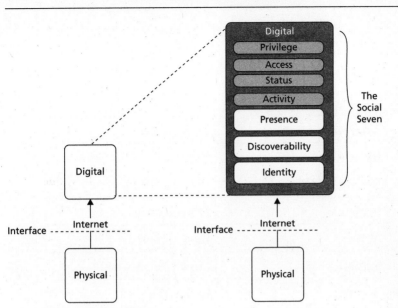

Figure 8.3 The Social Seven

As Figure 8.4 illustrates, there are seven basic characteristics that all social machines share.

Attribute	Description
Identity	A unique identifier for the network connection
Discoverability	The ability to get "looked up" on the network by another party or device
Presence	A flag indicating whether you are online and/or available for communication
Activity	A descriptor indicating your activity on a network
Status	A descriptor indicating your "posture" on the network
Access	The rights other network devices have to access your device
Privilege	The privileges granted to devices with access to your device

Figure 8.4 Social Seven Details

As foreign as these attributes may seem, they should all be familiar to you. We use them every day with a device that connects to one of the oldest network around: the telephone (Figure 8.5).

Attribute	Description
Identity	Your phone number
Discoverability	Are you listed?
Presence	Do you answer?
Activity	Busy signal?
Status	How you answer(!)
Access	Caller ID
Privilege	Custom ringtones

Figure 8.5   Normal Telephone Uses Social Seven

They are also the same attributes you assume when presenting yourself on an online network. It's probably become so natural to you that you don't give it a second thought, but let's examine what's happening. When you work with some of the Web's most popular tools, you are using the social seven. Take a look at Figure 8.6 and you'll see what I mean.

The great Creator of the human race did not include "Presence" or "Status" in the initial feature set. It was unnecessary. You were "present" when you were, well, present. But as soon as we started connecting ourselves together online, we recognized that these new digital characteristics, our avatar properties, became very valuable. In fact, in some cases (even legal cases), these properties are as important as our physical characteristics. For example, in October 2012, in the United

Application	Identity	Discoverability	Presence	Activity	Status	Access	Privilege
IM	X	X	X	X		X	
E-mail	X						
Facebook	X	X	X		X	X	X
Twitter	X	X					X

Figure 8.6   Social Seven Matrix

Kingdom, a 20-year-old man was imprisoned for three months for posting a Facebook status update that was deemed "grossly offensive"!

A few of these characteristics may be new to you. But they all represent rich areas for innovation and new thinking. It's no accident that we are concerned with the same issues that affect human communication over a network. After all, the whole point here is to bring machines into the mix. They will need to play by the rules, too. As a social machine product designer, you will need to be familiar with all the pros and cons of the social seven.

EXERCISE—Write down the number of ways you interacted with your friends, family, and colleagues before the days of the Internet. Now update that list with the ways you interact now. What are the new ways you could work with the objects in your life if you had similar access?

THE SOCIAL SEVEN—DETAILS

The following section will provide details on each of the seven attributes and describe their use in social machine design.

Identity

Figure 8.7   Identity

"The beginning of wisdom is to call things by their right names."

—Chinese proverb

Overview   The foundation stone for all network communication is identity. If you can't uniquely identify each network node, confusion reigns. This is not a new problem. Uniquely identifying people and things in a group is a challenge that's existed since the beginning of human history. We've come up with many systems to help out, in addition to just our family and proper names. There are social security numbers, driver's license numbers, passport numbers, employee IDs, credit card numbers, and so on. The goal of all these approaches was and is to associate the real, physical you with a totally unique, abstract alphanumerical sequence that could always and reliably be used to identify you, for whatever reason. It's something that we all take for granted but that becomes surprisingly complex when you need to start thinking about it from a design perspective. Why, I hear you asking, do I need to worry about identifying my product outside of the bar code on the box?! It's because your product will now become available online, and it will need a digital identity in addition to its physical one. In a similar fashion, I may be Peter Semmelhack when you meet me in person but PS20348 if we meet online.

Online identification poses interesting and occasionally maddening new challenges for the designer. Any online system that grants access to its platform requires some type of unique ID to participate (for example, a log-in). The trouble is, there is no way of proving that the unique ID reliably identifies anybody *real*. Sure, your name may be Mary and you live in Boston, but you could just as easily fill in the online registration form saying your name is Petunia and you live in Anchorage. Who's to know? The creation of a virtual identity has created all kinds of areas for innovation (and lots of opportunities for trouble as well). The game *Second Life* was based entirely on the idea of creating not only a new you, also called an avatar, but a whole new world in which your new avatar could "live" with other avatars. *World of Warcraft* has built an online gaming business allowing you to shed your human skin entirely and become an elf, an orc, or any of a number of other fantastical creatures. On the Internet you can be anything or anyone you want. In fact, you can have multiple personalities.

The same thing applies to objects. Take our social bicycle as an example. If you sell 10,000 bicycles, all of them capable of communicating on a network and sharing data, each one will need a unique ID to help sort out what data are coming from which bike. Users will want to log in to a website to view their own, and possibly their groups', riding stats. Physical products receive serial numbers. Social machines require a digital counterpart, an online identity, on which to base all that comes next. Bruce Sterling sums it up nicely.

> "Why would "identity" ever become "more important" than a real, no-kidding physical object? How is such a thing even possible? The answer is found in a new means of focusing society's attention and enabling joint effort.

> Only a limited number of people can interact with any particular physical object . . . The object's virtual representations, however, can have stakeholders. For instance, it makes more sense to own shares of a company than it does to own physical pieces of a company. Like shares of stock, models of an object can be shown and distributed to a wide public. The models are more open than real objects. The models can attract a huge amount of creative effort worldwide."

Implications for Product Design   Of all the seven attributes, identity is the most important. You can't design a social machine without a way to identify it on a network. Depending on the network type—Wi-Fi, cellular, or Bluetooth—there are nuances to how this is accomplished. Sound complicated? It doesn't have to be. In fact, it can be very straightforward if you consider what's necessary early enough in the design cycle. And, in the Resources section, I provide more information and links to helpful material.

Discoverability

Figure 8.8   Discoverability

Overview   How long did it take you to regret that on Facebook everyone could find you instantly? Was it when all your long-lost, high school semi-acquaintances suddenly discovered you and wanted to relive all those awkward teenage moments? Or when your old girlfriends or boyfriends started looking you up? Or when forgotten business colleagues started commenting on your wall with embarrassing anecdotes from a past you wished would stay buried? All of the above?

If any of these examples ring true, then you understand the importance of *discoverability*. Maybe the original Facebook designers didn't really give it enough thought. Or maybe they just didn't appreciate its power. Needless to say, it's a feature that has incredible utility. And with incredible utility comes incredible responsibility. Like the presence feature (see later discussion), including ways to list or delist your product from whatever network it's connected to is vitally important, especially if the data your product produces or consumes (or both) are confidential, personal, or sensitive in any way. It may be that the simple fact that *that* specific product is on the network *at all* is enough data to make a difference to someone or something. The flip side: It may be critical that as many other devices and/or people find your product as quickly as possible for it to be a success. You *want* visibility on the network and are not shy about sharing what you have with whoever discovers you.

Implications for Product Design   With POTS (plain old telephone system) lines, we have listed and unlisted numbers. Today, as a product designer, you need to decide how you want to play that game. Like many of the features listed here, a lot will depend on the context in which your product operates and what type of data it produces and/or consumes. But don't ever underestimate the importance of this key quality, as it could easily make or break the popularity of your design.

Presence

Figure 8.9   Presence

Overview   Do you remember the first time you used instant messaging? For many it was via America Online. If you were an uber-geek, you may have used IRC, or Internet relay chat. It was undeniably cool being able to have what amounted to a text-based, walkie-talkie-like discussion with anyone connected to the network, wherever he or she was on the planet. But there was another aspect of the instant messaging interface that became equally important and probably in ways the designers hadn't fully appreciated: this was the online presence indicator, the visual cue in the interface that told people whether you were online or not. It was an innocent, simple little feature, meant to be helpful to those looking to communicate with you. But it quickly became more complicated. Maybe I wanted to be "present" for some people and not others. Maybe I wanted the ability to never be "present" even while I was actively chatting with others. What seemed like a simple feature became "fraught" with subtlety and innuendo. "Is that person in my chat list really offline, or is he just avoiding me?"

How does the concept of presence affect connected social product design? As you might expect, it can be as simple or as complex as you'd like to make it. Machines don't have emotions, so you don't need to worry about their feelings getting hurt if they get ignored by other people or machines. On the other hand, you may need to consider how, when, where, or why users may want their devices to be "present" for others to see and interact with. Say, for example, you're designing a medical device. Some of the data it produces may be sensitive or have different contextual meaning based on time of day, user location, and so on. As a result, you may need to give users the capacity to decide who gets to see when they are online and ready to share information.

In some cases, the simple "present" data point is all that's needed from the device. The fact that it's online and doing its thing is the only indicator its user needs or wants. Continuing the medical device example, the fact that the machine is online may be all that's required to know that Grandma is taking her medicine. From a connected product design standpoint, this is one of the simplest engagement models, but powerful nonetheless. One could easily imagine a cloud application that simply needs a certain number of connected widgets to come online before it executes. The presence indicator, in this case, is all that's needed.

Implications for Product Design The importance of a presence feature in your product will depend on who or what is monitoring that signal and how it is controlled. If both the monitor and controller are machines, then the interaction model will be straightforward. On the other hand, if they are human, then you will need to worry about the subtlety and innuendo issues I brought up earlier. Do you give control of network presence to users? Can they override the feature and be online but publish presence data that says they aren't? These are the issues a social product designer needs to evaluate when considering a presence feature.

Activity

Figure 8.10   Activity

Overview   This is similar to that little piece of information that pops up in instant messaging applications like iChat or gChat that mentions if the other party is "Typing . . ." This feature seems innocuous enough, but we all know it has a richer meaning as well. Just the mere fact that it pops up quickly or doesn't is an indicator of something potentially important in the dialog. Maybe the other person is intentionally not responding quickly! What does that imply?

The activity indicator is pointless if machines are speaking with one another. Network protocols have lots of ways to manage this already. Where the activity indicator becomes important is when a social machine is interacting with a human. There's a reason many laptops have a little LED light that goes on when the hard drive is "working." Without it, it can seem like the computer has gone into slow motion with no warning.

Implications for Product Design   Activity alerts are very important for managing user expectations, which is critical for a good customer experience. Therefore, if a social machine is busy doing a complex task that's invisible to the user and will take some time, implementing a "Thinking . . ." or "I'm working on it . . ." activity notification may make sense.

Status

Figure 8.11   Status

Overview My understanding, appreciation, and horror of today's socially networked world took a quantum leap forward the day one of my colleagues got broken up with via a Facebook status update. There was no tragic face-to-face meeting, no teary, stuttering phone call ("It's not you; it's me!"). There was only the single, simple, devastating change of a word from "Attached" to "Single" on the significant other's Facebook page. I was blown away.

Machines don't have any emotions, so there is no trauma associated with status changes. But the power of the status indicator is still important with social machines—both when they are communicating with one another and when they are communicating with people. Obviously the meaning of the status indicator is of primary importance; for example, "Available" and "Do Not Disturb" are pretty self-explanatory. In addition, the time between status changes could be meaningful, or the sequence of status updates could indicate something important.

Implications for Product Design Status indicators are good for organizing and coordinating actions between machines and between machines and people. For example, if a group of online devices all need to reach a certain point, say, a location, before executing their next action, status indicators are a very easy way to organize that. They are also very effective for feedback loops, providing real-time responses to users and helping them interact more effectively.

Access

Overview   So your product is discoverable, identifiable, online, and active. Do you want just anyone to have complete access to all its features? At any time of day or night? For hours, days, or weeks at a time? To control all this you need access controls of some sort. The most common method of dealing with these issues is by installing a front door on the device—a log-in that requires authentication of some kind. Based on the log-in, you can then grant access to the device in whatever manner is appropriate. The log-in process is an important part of any security functions your social machine must support. And like the log-ins you use every day, they come in a variety of forms based on the level of security required and the computing capabilities of your product.

Figure 8.12   Access

Implications for Product Design If guarding access to your social machine on a network is important, then this characteristic may be the most critical of all. Various levels of access control can be used to create the right security profile for your device. For example, you can require log-ins at the network, application, and device levels. You can restrict access from the cloud or at the device itself (assuming it has the power to run applications on its own). Detailing all the possible security options is beyond the scope of this book (there are many), but suffice it to say, getting it right is important. I've included more information in the Resources section of this book.

Privileges

Figure 8.13   Privileges

Overview This is related to access in the sense that it controls who can do what once they are connected to your product. Maybe you want to have different levels of service provided based on a specific package the customer purchased. Or maybe you want to have a promotion that is timed to end at a certain point. These types of controls are called privileges and they can be created, modified, and deleted at any time with the appropriate . . . privileges! Access provides the keys to the building. Privileges control which floors the elevator will take you to.

Implications for Product Design Like access, privileges are important when security and privacy are important. And similar to access, you can implement controls at the network, application, and/or device levels. Privileges make sense when more than one type of user will be accessing the same device. For example, there may be users who can only view certain types of data, while others have full access 24 hours a day.

CHAPTER 9

Spheres of Use, or Why Your New Product Should Do Things You Never Envisioned

Abstracting your physical product into a series of services available on a network opens the door to further innovation by others. I hope I've convinced you of that by now. And to the extent it helps further engage your imagination, I think it helps to recognize that the way your product will be used may diverge somewhat, or entirely, from what you anticipated—which is a wonderful thing. Knowing that, the decisions you make at every level of product development may change. You might recognize that product features and functions that impede its free and open use should be scrutinized and reevaluated. Everything from licensing to documentation to application programming interface (API)/avatar design should be examined with an eye toward removing *friction*.

I mentioned in Part I that the metrics for product success should evolve to include more than just unit sales. Products should be graded, in part, by their *foundation* value. That is, how many others have used them to build upon and launch their own successes? What better way for social machines to contribute to society than to serve as cornerstones for its advancement? Figure 9.1 is a good illustration of the potential. You can't

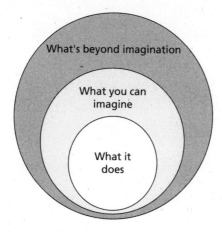

Figure 9.1   Social Machines Will Be Used in Unexpected Ways

possibly imagine every conceivable use of your product design (for example, my friend's young son uses his iPhone as a hammer!), and that shouldn't bother you too much. What you should concentrate on is making sure you remove as many barriers as possible to others' imagination, or even better, add a feature that entices it. One of my favorite examples of this is the Roomba, a little, autonomous robotic vacuum cleaner made by iRobot (www.irobot.com). Introduced in 2002, they have sold millions of units. But most important for this discussion, in 2005 the Roomba designers decided to include an electronic and software interface that, in essence, became a portal for third-party innovation. The designers installed this "door," opened it, and let the imaginations of the user community run wild. The results have been impressive. In fact, there's a website devoted to doing it— www.hackingroomba.com! The point is, good social machine design should include features that may not be immediately useful to primary customers but fire up the creative imaginations of developers. You never know what they will dream up and build.

PART III

The Business of Social Machines

Know the rules well, so you can break them effectively.
—*Dalai Lama XIV*

CHAPTER 10

Introduction

The business of social is the business of sharing. Research the business model for any social networking company, and you will see that its goal is to sell services to others based on the social sharing of its users. Facebook has Likes, Twitter has tweets, and Pinterest has pins. They are all a form of sharing—an activity the sites monetize in the form of advertising, promotions, and marketing services. But there are other services that can be built on top of sharing. I will review two in this chapter. Neither has to do with people sharing ideas, opinions, wants, or needs. They have to do with people sharing *things* and *things* sharing data. And they point the way for how to build businesses based on social machines, a topic we delve into in Chapter 11.

PEOPLE SHARING *THINGS*

As I write this, a new crop of start-ups are getting funded that focus on enabling what sounds like a fancy new collective behavior called *collaborative consumption*. In reality, it's just an easier way of allowing people and organizations to *rent, lend, swap*, and/or *barter* things they already own. It is billed as a way for owners to maximize their return on investment of an asset by expanding usage beyond just their own. It could be a house, a boat, a car, a tool, or even your skills or schedule. For customers it's a way to gain access to things/assets they don't own and pay for only what they use. Of course, this idea is not new in any real sense. People have been doing this sort of thing for ages. What makes it different now is the marketing and distribution mechanism powered by the Web and mobile apps. Today, you can instantly broadcast, worldwide, the availability and price of just about anything you own. Likewise, you can search the world over for things you'd like to rent, swap, and so on. Companies are building businesses that use the power of the Web to connect these new buyers and sellers in compelling and potentially lucrative new ways. And just like eBay and Craigslist discovered years ago, there's actually an active, vibrant market for it all. Turns out people are interested in sharing just about everything.

Accommodation Services—Airbnb

Perhaps the best known example of this new trend is the San Francisco–based company Airbnb (airbnb.com), a website that helps you easily rent out your house, apartment, or other accommodation (even just a room in your garage!) to others. Here's the blurb from its website:

> Airbnb is a trusted community marketplace for people to list, discover, and book unique accommodations around the world—online or from a mobile phone. Whether an apartment for a night, a castle for a week, or a villa for a month, Airbnb connects people to unique travel experiences, at any price point, in more than 26,000 cities and 192 countries.

This is a business built on helping you monetize what is usually one of your biggest investments: your dwelling. It's a radically simple, attractive concept—make good money in a safe, repeatable, new way while incurring very little cost. What's not to love about it? From our discussion's point of view, what's important is that Airbnb is not selling the asset itself. To participate in Airbnb you don't have to sell your apartment. You're selling only *access*. In fact, you're selling a *service*. Airbnb helps you sell *accommodation services* to others. As a seller, you list your property (your service) on its website and describe its features (location, attributes, etc.), the various conditions/constraints that help define the offering, and finally the price. It's a simple marketplace made possible by the power of the Internet and social networking. This idea has proved so popular that the high-flying Airbnb is, as of this writing, providing its service in 26,000 cities in 192 countries worldwide. Clearly, the idea of maximizing the value of one's assets is hugely attractive.

But listing your accommodation service is only one side of the equation. Let's look at the other, equally important transaction component: the customers. Why are they flocking to Airbnb and handing over their hard-earned money to rent accommodations in new places from complete strangers? What unmet need has Airbnb discovered and satisfied? In a word, choice. And to consumers, choice rules. Airbnb has an enormous inventory of rentable properties that no hotel can match. They are the international supermarket in a world of corner delicatessens. You want a tiny little bungalow on the beach in Cancun? Check. A penthouse apartment on New York's Central Park? Check. An entire island in the Bahamas? No problem. The Airbnb platform provides customers with a staggering catalog of possibilities, which provides them a significant, difficult-to-duplicate competitive advantage.

But that's only part of the answer. The last piece is pricing, which can be tricky since customers are buying a *service* (not a thing) and paying for actual usage only. Airbnb uses an exchange mechanism to unlock the inherent, latent value that exists in the unused or underutilized assets that we own. It provides liquidity in a previously illiquid market—all accessible via a standard Web interface and rentable using an easily understood transaction model. Airbnb's success is not based on an innovative new business idea. It's based on the power of networks to connect people in new ways. Airbnb's strengths revolve around market transparency—who's selling and buying what *right now*—and removing market friction by introducing easy-to-use and easy-to-understand technologies to match up buyers and sellers. Since it doesn't actually own any of the properties listed, it resembles a brokerage and receives brokerage-like fees. But because its brokering tools are accessed via connected online computers, Airbnb can offer the latest availability, pricing, and ecosystem data to *anyone*, not just professionals. Buyers and sellers of all stripes get the same attention. This dynamic creates an incredibly valuable, virtuous cycle. Sellers list their properties on Airbnb because that's where all the buyers are. Conversely, buyers visit the site and search for accommodations because that where all the sellers are—and that's where they'll find the most choice. Suffice to say, companies that find themselves in this fortunate position gain many advantages. The key is to uncover market areas that could benefit from the same technical and economic approach. Social machines, by definition, should be obvious candidates for markets like these. As we've already discussed, social machines are all about data and therefore easily shared. The opportunities are easily addressed with available technology.

Transportation Services—Zipcar

In 2000, Antje Danielson and Robin Chase cofounded a car-sharing company called Zipcar (zipcar.com). It was based on successful German and Swiss car-sharing models and has become a huge hit here in the United States. Unlike traditional car rental companies, Zipcar has no central garages and no rental offices where you stand in line to sign an agreement, get your keys, say no to the fuel option, and drive off. Zipcar doesn't require any of that expensive overhead. Instead, it is based on a membership model. Members pay an annual fee and receive a special card that identifies them and their payment information. The card also includes a special electronic RFID tag (radio-frequency identification tag) that uniquely identifies the card and, therefore (ideally!), its user. The cars themselves are equipped with special computers that keep track their whereabouts, operational statistics, and log travel and user information. The computer also serves another critical function: It unlocks the doors. Zipcar members don't behave like normal car renters. Instead of a central garage, members looking to use a car go to designated parking lots or streets where other members have left them prior.

To use the car, the member produces his or her RFID-tagged card and waves it in front of a special area on the windshield. The computer identifies the user as a legitimate member and unlocks the doors. Ideally, there is a full tank of gas waiting for you (members are encouraged to tank up when they're finished—the cost is included in the rental and it's just a polite thing to do), you start up, and take off. When you're done, you return the car to either where you got it or some other designated spot in the neighborhood. Again, the computer keeps track of it and lets other members know where to find it. I'm a New Yorker, and when I first heard that the model was based on what amounts to a good Samaritan approach to sharing expensive things like cars, I was skeptical. But, happily, I was dead wrong. People enjoy the flexibility, freedom, and choice the model provides and, in the vast majority of the cases, are happy to play by the rules to maintain the privilege. As a telling example, the Zipcars available in my area are not shoddy old Fords and Chevys. They are new BMWs, Mini Coopers, and other fun, useful vehicles. Again, not at all what I would have expected.

Like Airbnb, Zipcar capitalizes on the idea that sometimes *things* are better viewed as *services*. It helps everyone maximize value. If you go read Robin Chases's blog (which I highly recommend) at robinchase.org, you'll find that one of her main goals at Zipcar, and at most of the things she has pursued since, is to "find and make use of excess capacity." She continues: "The opportunity here is boundless, really. And at every level of the economy. We all want to get more out of what we own or have already invested in, or, conversely, to pay only for what we use." Notice how she nicely summarizes the benefits to both buyer and seller. She also paints a picture that I will reiterate myself: The business opportunities for this type of thinking are enormous. She has already started up her new venture in France called Buzzcar, a "service that brings together owners and drivers in a car sharing marketplace," which continues to expand the possibilities of what Craig Newmark of Craigslist fame defines as "people using the Internet to work together in the service of one another."

Her work has inspired many others. Already just in the automobile space alone there are a wealth of innovative approaches. Zimride (zimride.com) in the United States helps you find rides to wherever you want to go. It is, almost literally, the latest form of hitchhiking, inspired and enabled by the Internet. Want to get from San Francisco to San Diego? There's a car leaving tomorrow at 2 PM and there's one seat left for $55! Zimride allows you to maximize the value of the empty seats in your car, which for many people go empty a majority of the time. ParkatmyHouse (parkatmyhouse.com) actually lets you rent out your driveway! I think you get the point.

There are other examples, too. You can share bikes, tools, textbooks, art pieces, fashion items, electronics, movies, and, yes, sewing machines. You can rent out your time (taskrabbit.com), your money (prosper.com), and your skills (skillshare.com). There is even a site dedicated to the movement—collaborative-consumption.com, which lists all the possibilities. As I mentioned earlier, none of this is exactly new. Nothing has stopped you from doing any of this before. The difference now is the real-time visibility of market participants. Buyers and sellers can now easily participate in exchanges that encourage and reward sharing. The other crucial difference is the social element. By using the power of social networks to disseminate messages, there is a geometric increase in the velocity of information flows—a huge benefit to the efficiency of any exchange.

THINGS SHARING DATA

We just reviewed how organizations can find new value selling services based on sharing *things*, and how social machines (as things themselves) are perfectly suited for being shared as well. This next section is how we can create things, *social machines*, that share data.

Financial Services—Progressive Insurance

A great example of this concept revolves around a pricing model called "pay as you go." As the name implies, its primary attraction is the idea that you, as a customer, don't pay a fixed price for a product. You pay for your actual usage of it "as you go." You can now rent books from Amazon and pay your town a trash fee based on the actual weight of your garbage. This, by itself, isn't a new concept, of course. But when it's applied to certain products, very interesting possibilities arise—for example, insurance.

When you combine the pay-as-you-go model with auto insurance you get something called a pay-as-you-drive policy, and Progressive Insurance is at the forefront of this new product category. Progressive sells a type of usage-based insurance with rates based on both the quality and the quantity of your driving. That is, you pay less if you drive well and drive less.

To participate in this program, you need to plug a little black box full of electronics, called the Snapshot, into your car's diagnostic port (officially, the OBD-II port), normally located in the wheel well just under the steering wheel. Once installed, the Snapshot monitors and logs information about your driving and transmits it to Progressive for analysis and reporting. For example, the device will detect sudden acceleration and deceleration via its built-in accelerometer. It will record vehicle speed and time information as well as when the device is connected and disconnected from the car by monitoring information coming from the diagnostic port (from which it also gets its power). It does not track location via GPS, although Progressive mentions in its terms and conditions that it could probably determine your approximate whereabouts, with your permission (!) by triangulating your position via the cell phone towers the Snapshot communicates with.

On the surface, we would all like to believe that we're safe drivers and deserve a break on our insurance, and in most cases, we'd probably be correct. Today, insurance companies have no choice but to use complicated actuarial models for their pricing. They have little idea what financial risk you personally pose to them as an institution. But by agreeing to get tracked, you receive the opportunity to prove it. Progressive's approach has been successful enough that other insurance companies are beginning to offer similar plans. It's an obvious win-win for both parties.

There is another, less obvious, secondary benefit to this approach as well. Certainly, you should get a break on your premiums if you drive more safely than the next guy. But shouldn't you also get a break if you drive *less?* Yes, you should. In fact, the statistics back that up. The more you drive, the more likely it is that you'll get into an accident. Check out the chart in Figure 10.1.

The graph makes it clear that insurance companies would prefer if you drove less because it would equal fewer accidents. In fact, the variable insurance premium starts to resemble a tax. And like a tax, it serves as a powerful disincentive to drive. So insurance companies can now play a role in the greening of the planet by creating financial incentives for creating less pollution.

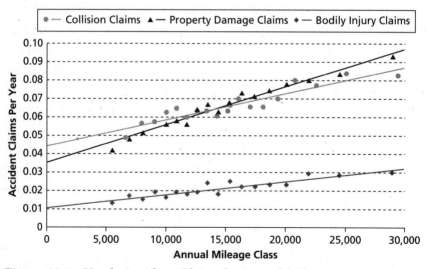

Figure 10.1   Yearly Accident Claims by Annual Mileage
Source: Hamilton Project, July 2008

This clever trick is an example of something called behavioral economics, which we'll come back to in the next example.

Whether Progressive realizes it or not, the Snapshot is much more than just a simple, wireless monitoring device. It's a platform-enabler with far-reaching impact because it can *share* data, the basis for social value creation. It opens the door to creating a truly social interaction. What other products could Progressive build on this platform? More important, what products could others build if given the chance? It's not hard to imagine a world where this platform gives Progressive the opportunity to offer entirely new categories of product, from location-based promotions to performance-based deals on goods and services of interest to specific drivers. After all, Progressive knows quite a bit about you and your car.

Progressive is much more than an automobile insurance company. According to its website, the company also insures homes, health, life, pets, and classic cars. It would be easy to envision the pay-as-you-go model working with most, if not all, of their other product lines.

Take health, for example. It would make perfect sense for an active, nonsmoking, healthy-eating, and conscientious customer to pay less for health insurance than someone who is not all those things. Taking the Snapshot example one step further, it's not hard to imagine a scenario where someone trades the ability to track his or her daily habits in return for lower premiums. The social machine construct provides a good way to envision how this could work. Health device makers could easily provide secure interfaces to their products that allow remote access to authorized users. The devices themselves could post relevant information to insurance company databases or social networks. Third-party developers could offer applications that simultaneously help users live healthier, more active lives and provide insurance companies with the data they need to keep rates low.

You could even imagine pay-as-you-go insurance for pets with connected collars, health monitors, trackers, and so on, providing the required data to owners and insurance companies alike.

Health Services—Vitality, Inc.

Another interesting thing happens when you connect devices into our social fabric. Companies are finding business opportunities helping us do the "right thing"—driving more safely, staying healthy, protecting the environment. By using a collection of principles from the field of behavioral economics, companies are using data from connected devices to create compelling win-win scenarios for both their customers and themselves.

A good example of a company using these principles is Vitality, Inc. (vitality.net). This company develops and markets a product called GlowCaps, an innovative, wirelessly connected pill bottle cap that broadcasts to your social network whether you've been taking your medicine (or not!).

Here's what a *Wall Street Journal* article said about them:

Vitality Inc., a Cambridge, Mass., start-up, wants to apply behavioral economics to prompt people to take prescriptions. Vitality's GlowCaps use lights and sounds as reminders. The caps also contain a radio transmitter that sends e-mail to doctors, relatives, and others about how often the cap is opened.

Mr. Ariely says people are more likely to take medicines as prescribed if they believe others are watching—an idea not addressed in typical economic theory. "Why should you care about what other people do? It's irrelevant," to a classical economist, Mr. Ariely says. But not to a behavioral economist.

Vitality President Josh Wachman hopes to market the GlowCaps to drug makers, pharmacies, insurers, and patients, arguing they will improve compliance and save money by preventing more costly health problems.

Like the auto insurance example, this product produces a win-win situation based purely on the data flowing from the connected device. And similarly, because the GlowCaps have the ability to share data, there are significant opportunities for further innovation by Vitality itself and, more important, third-party innovators as well.

There are other good examples as well. As I mentioned in Chapter 1, companies like Nike and Adidas are building fitness products and online portals designed to share the performance metrics of their users. Automobile manufacturers like Ford, GM, Audi, and BMW have announced products that are Internet-connected and capable of sharing operating information. Soon there won't be a product you will consider that is not somehow connected and capable of being woven into your social network.

CHAPTER **11**

How to Build a Business Using
Social Machines

RETROFIT MODEL

Many companies, such as those discussed in Chapter 10, are creating a new service layer on top of an existing class of assets just by connecting them to the Internet—Progressive via a black box attached to your car and GlowCaps via a cap on a standard medicine bottle. They are driving new revenue streams from existing *things*. I call it the *retrofit model*. This business approach has the advantage of an existing target market—for example, there are hundreds of millions of cars in the United States. This is great if, for example, you want to start a new, socially connected car-sharing service in your area. Because all U.S. cars share a standard OBD-II port (the same one that Progressive uses), you can build one "black box" that connects customer cars to the Internet and enables the sharing of data. What it shares specifically is up to you (recall the discussion in Part II). But the point is that a single product investment allows you to retrofit a large, existing market.

Let's use the same thinking with the Airbnb example from Chapter 10.

For Airbnb to work, it needs a large inventory of houses, apartments, and other forms of accommodation. To accomplish that, the company needs to convince you that your house is worth putting on its system because it will generate interest and therefore income for you. But for most of us, our houses are not rent-ready. As a potential Airbnb customer, you start to think about how you'll need to *retrofit* your home. I can tell you from personal experience that the notion of strangers staying in your home causes you to think about things in entirely new ways. You'll want to look around and make sure you have a good way to secure valuables, remove or hide your special things (such as photos), set up insurance coverage, fix things you've always put off repairing, and so on. In effect, you start to look at your house like a product developer keen on satisfying a customer. You want the service you're providing to be good. You want it to represent your *brand* properly. In the end, you want to charge as much as possible for it! So it has to be great. The best Airbnb sellers are motivated retrofitters.

To help you with this process, it's not hard to imagine Airbnb working with device makers to develop a line of Airbnb-certified products that, if used in your house, apartment, and so on, gave you some pricing edge on their system. Sellers can *retrofit* their properties with special devices to make them more social and therefore more attractive and popular. Conversely, homes equipped with such devices could provide quality assurances of various kinds to the buyers. What kinds of devices would make sense? Think about these for a minute:

- *Access systems:* Like Zipcar, properties equipped with Airbnb-certified access systems would allow the holders of special cards to gain easy access to their rentals. All parties would benefit. Sellers would have an easy-to-manage way to control access to their property and could view reports on usage. Buyers would also receive a trusted, easy-to-use access method. Device makers could take advantage of a budding new market. And Airbnb would strengthen its ties to its customers and suppliers while simultaneously improving the "stickiness" of its offerings, hence improving its competitiveness.

  Why is this social? Access systems could tie into the Airbnb website, offering usage dashboards for property owners. Systems could also post usage on social networks or enterprise systems in real time. Accessing participating properties could equate to check-ins that earn reward points and other benefits.

- *Security systems:* These are similar to access systems. In fact, they could work together. Suppliers who install

Airbnb-certified security systems could receive lower fees, greater search visibility, and/or promotional opportunities. Buyers could feel better renting a property with these systems installed. Airbnb could derive a savings in insurance costs from their suppliers.

Why is this social? Communities could monitor themselves. Security breaches could instantly post messages, send tweets, make phone calls, and so forth.

- *HVAC systems:* Makers of *social* heaters, air conditioners, dehumidifiers, and so on, would all benefit from the Airbnb certification program. Using the real-time dashboards that could be made available on the Airbnb site, both buyers and sellers could understand their energy use. Sellers could set up models where they charge buyers for usage. Customers would benefit because there would be no billing surprises. Manufacturers could benefit by receiving usage reports back from Airbnb along with diagnostic data that could help them improve their product development. In addition, Airbnb could offer low-cost maintenance services to certified sellers because they would have a very clear view of the status of the machines on a monthly basis. Airbnb, like the other examples, benefits by offering up valuable new ways to engage with buyers and sellers.

  Why is this social? Energy usage could be shared and reported to utilities in return for discounts on energy bills. Usage triggers could be set to tweet or SMS if specific thresholds are exceeded.

We examined only two markets in these examples, but I hope it shows how the retrofit model is a great way to explore a market with the social machine lens. It allows you to take an existing asset, add connectivity and smarts, and start benefiting from sharing the data.

BUILT-IN MODEL

The retrofit model makes sense in the short term, but the more enduring, and I argue, more fundamental approach is to design devices to be social from the beginning. I call this approach the built-in model, and it is already beginning to happen. Companies are actively redesigning their products with network connectivity in mind. For example, most of the major automakers are already responding to the car-sharing boom by publicly talking about designing cars that are *built for sharing*. That's a huge step forward and a key milestone in social product design.

To discuss how the built-in model works, I'll use a hypothetical HVAC company called HighlyCool AC, which is, hypothetically, looking to build a new air conditioner. I'll walk through the necessary questions and steps to begin designing and developing a *social* AC unit. The key point to remember here is what we learned in the earlier chapters: A product is nothing more than *data*. Keep that in mind while we go through the example.

Scenario

HighlyCool AC, Inc. is a manufacturer of high-quality residential and commercial air-conditioning units.

Its mission: to find new ways to drive energy efficiency and "green" features to increase profit margins and improve competitive positioning while improving the customer experience.

The traditional approach to tackling the stated mission would be to focus inward on the product itself, its components and physical design. We would look for improved performance from our suppliers on both product specs and cost. We would place enormous importance on end users as we tried to understand, predict, and address their needs. We do this because once we've made the final decisions on new features and functions, they are, in fact, *final*. Once the new product is manufactured and distributed, you can't go back and say, "Oops, I really wanted to include *x*." So hitting the customer requirements mark is essential. Most likely, we'd be looking to create a new version of the current successful model. But inevitably, we would be looking at a 12-month minimum new product introduction cycle. Maybe we could do better than that, but on average, that's the reality of it. And this makes it even more challenging, because what we're trying to do is not just understand our customers' needs today but to figure out what those needs will be a year in the future. Given the pace of change and soaring demands of customers, this entire process is becoming untenable.

There's a different way to handle this challenge as well (no surprise—isn't that the whole point of this book?). I'm tempted to say it's a better approach, but it's not always. The traditional method of improving products has a long history and its precepts and results are well known. The *social* method of approaching this product development challenge is to turn our focus inside out. We will pay less attention to improving what's inside the box and more on how we can radically improve the ways that box interacts with things and people who are *outside* of it.

Remember, a social product is all about *data*. The goal is to identify, package, and present these data in a way that benefits everyone. Step 1 is to focus inward and see what data might be available from within the air conditioner itself.

Potential Data from the AC Unit

- Physical dimensions
- Manufacturing date and location
- Bill of materials
- Power status—full, energy saver, sleep, off, etc.
- Temp settings—from just a fan to full arctic blast
- Filter status—clear, getting dirty, completely clogged
- Timer settings

There are more, but let's limit it to this list for now.

Step 2 is to focus outward. This is the fun part. Ask yourself (and anyone else who has an opinion), these three questions:

1. How would having access to this air-conditioning data help others? Put a list together of who they might be, for example, end users, installers, maintainers/repairers, manufacturers, contractors, caregivers, and anyone who could possibly interact either with it or the environment in which it operates.

2. What *external* sources of data could make it easier, more efficient, more convenient, and/or more fun to own, use, and experience this air conditioner?

3. How can you make the data sources, both internal and external, easily available for third parties to use so that they can add value to your product on their own? How do you package it up and make it irresistible to other innovative minds? These questions revolve around the concept we introduced earlier. Remember, with a social machine there are three sets of customers—the primary customer, the developer, and the developer's customers.

Let's now answer these questions and see where it takes us.

1. I don't know about you, but I can immediately think of a lot of reasons why tons of people would benefit from having access to the product and operational data produced by an air conditioner. I will list a few.

   Customer: This is the low-hanging fruit. By connecting the air conditioner to a network, you allow remote access to it. I think it's fairly obvious why, for example, an iPhone app that gave you the ability to view the air conditioner's operational data would be handy. I think it is completely obvious why giving you *control* over your air conditioner remotely via your smartphone would be super valuable. You could adjust its setting from across the room or across the yard. You could set up timers and other thresholds using apps running on your smartphone. You could run reports showing usage patterns over time. There are many things you could do with this approach to improve the user's experience.

2. It turns out that running your air conditioner can easily become the largest component of your monthly electric bill (percentage-wise). So anything you can do to reduce that amount would most likely be desirable. How could the air conditioner's operating data plus some *external* sources of data help you do that? If you look at it from the social machines, point of view, the answer, unsurprisingly, revolves around sharing. What if your utility company could monitor your usage in real time? What would that access enable it to do, and why should the customer care?

   This is a great example of how sharing creates a strong win-win situation. The utility company wins because it has a vested interest in understanding, as precisely as possible, who is using what energy and where. The company is incentivized to drive efficiencies. If customers would share their real-time usage data with the utility company, it could react in ways that would help the customers load balance much more effectively. The utility company could identify longer-term trends that would allow customers to take proactive, curative steps. For example, it could send customized e-mails to users suggesting things like cleaning filters or adjusting settings. It could even utilize game dynamics to motivate customers by offering free service in return for efficient air conditioner usage. From the customers' perspective it's a win because they pay less for the same level of service.

Combining individual air conditioner operating data with the usage statistics of the larger community is a great example of the power of social machines.

3. The best way to think of this is to imagine you're an application developer. Try on different hats and see what you come up with. Let's say we work for an HVAC maintenance company that services the equipment in apartment buildings in the local neighborhood. Let's further imagine we recognize that the more we know about our customers and their usage of the equipment we service, the easier it will be for us to be responsive and, therefore, more competitive. We notice that HighlyCool is selling an easy-to-use social machine interface on its latest AC units and write a Web application that can monitor the data from these machines in real time. Next, we offer this Web application as a dashboard to HighlyCool users and offer discounted pricing on maintenance for anyone who signs up. As a result, both the dashboard and lower pricing allow our company to offer a more valuable customer experience and compete more aggressively in what is normally a commodity service business. From here there are several interesting possibilities:

- Sell access to more premium features of the dashboard
- Develop additional applications for sale to customers
- Sell application IP to HighlyCool for a lot of money

How does all this equate to business models? The answers are intriguing.

Let's apply the concept that Airbnb and Zipcar use to the air conditioner. Is there a service layer that could get applied to that existing asset a basis for pricing valuable, innovative new functions? Here's a list of some possibilities:

- Charge fee for actual usage—pay-as-you-go model

- Access to data within a community—behavioral economics says people will compete to lower usage

- Access to usage data for manufacturers—data for improving the user experience (change the filter!) and improving product development

- Access to usage data for a utility—helps it manage capacity

- Access to operating data for a health provider—improves conditions for occupants who may be sensitive to temperature and humidity changes

- Access to data for a repair provider/maintainer—receive preventive maintenance, not emergency service, bills and get discounts on upgrades

What's great about these new approaches is they are separate from the asset itself. They are digitally based and can therefore continue to improve over time, enhancing customer value and increasing the product's life span. Social machines fit into this paradigm perfectly, as they are meant to be built on.

CHAPTER 12

My Customer's Customer Is My Customer

The Beauty of a Social Value Chain

The HighlyCool example in Chapter 11 demonstrates one of the most interesting and compelling business ideas that is enabled by social machines. As we discussed in Part II, a correctly designed social machine not only satisfies the needs of its intended Primary Customers but forms the foundation for third-party developers to build their own customer base using the data produced by that machine. This two-tiered model has interesting business ramifications.

Let's say HighlyCool releases their new social air conditioner, targeting owners of collaborative consumption business models like Airbnb, with a well-documented application programming interface (API) and sample applications for third-party developers to get their feet wet. Now imagine an entrepreneurial person or organization decides to write an application that lets owners of the new HighlyCool AC unit charge for its use (say, by the minute). It's a simple mobile application that keeps track of each machine's usage (it can do this because of Social Seven properties we discussed in Part II) and produces itemized bills on-demand for the user. Payment could be handled by a mobile payment system such as Square (square.com).

This application could also allow HighlyCool's customers to pay only for "cooling services," meaning they could receive the AC unit itself for no charge but would be required to pay periodic usage charges. This is a model that has been popular in the office equipment business for years. You don't pay for the copier itself. You pay for the copies it produces—that is, you are paying for the *service* of copying.

HighlyCool benefits from the three customer types.

- Primary customers—traditional buyers of AC units
- Developers—third-party developers who bring new value to the customer experience

- Developers' customers—new buyers for the AC unit that are attracted to the pay-as-you-go model

If you compare this model with that of today's current air conditioner manufacturers I think it's safe to say the thought process for this product development approach is quite different. It puts as much value on the product's social potential as it does on the normally required air conditioner features and functions. HighlyCool is betting that the social value of its products will not only provide an immediate and sustainable competitive edge, it will help position the company advantageously with the most important and influential community of all developers.

This is a great example of the types of business opportunities that can quickly arise once you add social characteristics to a product. The sharing of data instantly opens up new ways of devising business models, interacting with customers, and expanding your market.

CHAPTER 13

The Art of Social Pricing

Traditionally, when you make a *thing*, your goal is to sell that *thing* on the market. You figure out your cost of goods, determine what you want for margins, look at the competition, and set your price. It's pretty straightforward. But if you are a social machine developer and your device can share valuable data that could be useful to others on the network, then the revenue-generating opportunities expand. You can start to develop pricing models that take into account that users may buy additional services from you. I'll return to the Amazon Kindle as a good example. The price of the device is so attractively low not because Amazon has figured out how to significantly lower its manufacturing costs. It's because Amazon anticipates that you will load up your Kindle with content from the Amazon catalog, which, of course, it makes money on via each download. Amazon even covers the cost of 3G wireless airtime in this fashion, cutting the carrier into the revenue streams coming from these downloads.

Social machine designers have the same opportunities to price their products creatively. In the HighlyCool example from earlier, access to the product's application programming interface (API) was free, but that doesn't have to be the case. You could charge a licensing fee. Or you could make it available for no charge but limit the access to only a subset of the machine's available data. More comprehensive data sets could be accessed for an additional fee. You could also make everything available for free to developers and charge only *their* customers for access. This is yet another example of why it's important to understand the three customer types. The developer's customers open up whole new ways to think about pricing. Especially when you consider that the model allows your developer customer to potential add a new source of revenue to *their* business. As we saw in Chapter 12 with the HighlyCool example, there's nothing stopping their developer customers from charging for the product data streams they may have enhanced (e.g., via visualizations or analytics) with their applications.

In Part VI, you will read more about the creative ways social machines are helping businesses create new sources of revenue and engaging new users in mutually profitable relationships.

PART IV

Getting Started

When we change the way we communicate,
we change society.

—*Clay Shirky*, author of *Here Comes Everybody:
The Power of Organizing Without Organizations*

Chapter 14

Design Requirements

What Does It Take to Actually Design and Build a Social Machine?

In all of the examples discussed so far in this book, I glossed over the mechanics of actually designing and building a social machine. What does it really take to make it happen? What are the issues you need to concern yourself with to take a product and make it social? There are plenty of good books that discuss every aspect of electronic product development (see the Resources section for a list of some of my favorites), but I will lay out what basic requirements, issues, and challenges you will face as you embark on your *social* design. If you are an experienced electronic hardware designer, most of the lessons and suggestions I make will be familiar, with the exception perhaps of how they apply to a design focused on a social feature set. I've tried to highlight those points to make it easier to find them. Another thing to keep in mind is that many of the obstacles we face today will fade as Moore's law continues to work its magic, bringing costs down and making it easier to include computing power and network communications in more and more designs.

BUT FIRST, A QUICK STORY . . .

I include this story here because I think it's instructional. I want you to learn from my mistakes, because I've made quite a few. I boil the issues down into three lessons. These are the things I wish someone had drilled into my head before I started. Hence, I am presenting them to you in the hopes that you can use them to your advantage. This story is meant primarily for those readers who are entrepreneurs, business leaders, product developers, and/or designers who have never built electronic hardware before.

I started Bug Labs in 2006 with the idea of bringing to the world of electronic hardware what had been so successful with software—the concept of open source IP. There were others just getting started then, too, the most famous of which is Arduino.

There was Openmoko, a Taiwanese company hoping to make an open source cell phone; Chumby, which was an open source desktop media player wrapped in a cuddly ball; and us. That was pretty much it in 2006. Google search "open source hardware" today and you get a different result. But all of us held, as a core belief, that if you could democratize the process by which hardware got designed and brought to market, you could materially increase the pace and lower the costs of innovation. Instead of praying to St. Jobs to build you the gadget of your dreams, you could just go do it yourself—DIY. The analogy was solid. Just like the world witnessed with open source software, great things happen when you democratize the innovation process. But first we needed to build it.

Although my entire career had been spent in the software business, I grew up building Heathkits with my father. If you're not familiar with them (which means you were born after 1975), they were very well designed and documented electronics kits for building things like radios, televisions, stereos, and other types of geekery. In fact, if you search eBay for them, you will find many even today. They just worked (and still do). I was good with a soldering iron, etching fluid, and wire strippers. So in 2005 I had a modern notion of software IP but a 1970s conception of hardware. When I began thinking about starting Bug Labs, I assumed that the hardware world must have changed and advanced like the software industry. Imagine my astonishment when I discovered that nothing, in fact, had really changed. There had obviously been huge leaps forward in chip design regarding both of power and miniaturization over the prior 30 years, but for an individual hardware hacker trying to build something innovative and new, it felt like the Heathkits days. You still needed a soldering iron, etching fluid, and wire strippers.

So I managed to convince Union Square Ventures (more about them in the Resources section) to fund my dream and off we went to change the world. We had big plans and endless optimism. New York City was humming with new start-ups. It was around this time that I heard this quote from the famous German general Helmuth von Moltke:

No battle plan survives contact with the enemy.

It's a great quote because it's so true and not just on the battlefield. Bug Labs had big plans and ambitious launch dates . . . but fate had other ideas.

I could spend many pages going through all the difficult lessons a software guy learns in the land of hardware development, but I will instead distill it down into a sentence you hear all the time in this environment. *Hardware is hard.* That's not meant to be a warning or a threat. It's meant only as a helpful hint. It's so important that I will make point of calling it out again.

Lesson 1—Hardware Is Hard

Such an easy three words to say! But how is it hard?

The basic, immutable issue that underlies all hardware development, and distinguishes it from software development, is simple economics. With hardware you're dealing with atoms. With software, you're working with bits. And because you're dealing with physical things and not digital ephemera, you are subject to the same forces that drive all markets—scarcity. When building your next killer iPhone app, you will never need to worry about a shortage of bits. There will never be a six-month wait for IF . . . THEN statements. On the other hand, it is very likely that you will encounter shortages of integrated circuits, resistors, diodes, and/or connectors. You will find that scheduling time at the facility that produces your hardware is not on-demand. You will develop newfound respect for distributors and other brokers who will continue to support the chip you've included in the design but just went EOL (end of life). You will realize how easy you had it in a world without all this physical and temporal *friction*. And most likely, you will achieve all this enlightenment while you are trying desperately to hit a deadline. If you sense some tension in my writing it's because just thinking about it again is making me anxious! But you can learn from this. Bottom line: The world of hardware has many points of friction that impact everything you do. As a result, your scheduling needs to accommodate this.

I was reminded of all these issues when I recently read this blog post headline:

Would You Rather Have 10 Angry Investors or 68,000?

Here's a segment from the article:

It came out last week that star Kickstarter* project Pebble—the highest raiser on the site—had failed to ship their 85,000 e-paper watches on time to their donors/customers, without any explanation or new expected ship date.

This prompted a little party in the "Comments" section, now at over 8,000 remarks . . .

The Pebble, as you may have surmised from this blurb, is an electronic watch. It has a cool e-paper display and communicates with your iPhone or Android phone via Bluetooth. If you go and peruse their blog, you will see that building it has been *problematic*. It was supposed to ship September 2012. As I write this in December, there is still no ship date announced. I have been in this exact same position and it is torture. My best guess for when

---

*Kickstarter is a very popular new way for innovative new projects, products, and ideas to get funding. It's based on a crowdsourcing model and is who funded Pebble. Their project was so successful it attracted more than 68,000 "investors" who contributed, basically, the cost of the watch, approximately $150. Yes, they've raised more than $10 million! I provide more detail on Kickstarter in the Resource section.

they'll ship, just based on my own experiences, is spring 2013—a six- to seven-month delay. My hats off to their whole team for working through it all. *Hardware is hard.*

Lesson 2—Any Disruption in the Development of Your Product Will Have 3× Greater Impact on Your Schedule Than You Anticipate

There isn't an electronics company on Earth that has not suffered from this problem. It's hard to build a schedule when you are trying to account for something that could radically rearrange it. But what this lesson is meant to emphasize is the following. When you sense trouble (notice I didn't say "if"), react decisively. React aggressively. Because in absence of bold action, your planning will suffer even further. Everything in hardware takes time, usually much more than you want. So acting quickly, at the very least, salvages the time you would likely waste wringing your hands or hoping for the best. I know this from firsthand experience.

Lesson 3—Don't Underestimate the Scheduling Impact of Certifications, Especially If You Need the Carriers to Support Your Product

The last piece of advice I will give represents a few of the deeper scars on my back. It has to do with certifications. This is yet another area that confounded my software industry–trained mind. Hardware products that contain certain components need to get certified by the Federal Communications Commission, or FCC, before they can be sold. If you want to sell your gadget in Europe, you'll need to get it CE certified. For the rest of the world, there are other certifications necessary. The point is, it's another obstacle. And it's a black box—a terrifying prospect for any planner with a tight schedule. You go in but you might not come out (certified, that is). This is what happened to us.

Our designers assured us that our product would sail through the FCC certification process. It didn't. Granted, our design was a very complicated and compact piece of technology but that failure—although we *did* try to have a backup plan just in case—threw our entire schedule down the toilet. Instead of immediately biting the bullet and finding a comprehensive solution, we tried to save time by applying design Band-Aids. It was not successful. See Lesson 2.

There is another set of certifications, too, if you're building a wireless product that you hope to have work on any of the public cellular wireless carriers' networks. These tests are meant to protect the network and its users from radios that transmit in ways that disrupt other users on the network, resulting in dropped calls, corruption of data, and other quality-of-service issues. Like the FCC certifications, these tests are a black box: You either pass, or your don't. But unlike the FCC, which tests for emissions from fairly well-understood sources—oscillators, diodes, and so on—wireless certifications test explicitly for radio emissions, which, so it seems, no one understands! "It's a black art!" is a line you will assuredly hear if you attempt to pass PTCRB and carrier network testing. I'm being overly dramatic, of course, but it is amazing how much effort needs to go into the design to make sure these tests are accounted for and passed. There is a good reason why many times, when you open up a cell phone, or anything else with a radio in it, you see the circuit board completely covered with a shiny, thin sheet of metal. It's called a shield, and it's an inelegant, blunt, but quick way to deal with radio emissions. Just bury them! Which is fine. You just need to account for that approach in your design and leave room for it in the assembly. We used this approach successfully at Bug Labs—but not before we failed several times over!

These are the main lessons I seek to impart upon you. There are many more, but these are the ones that stand out as the most relevant and practical. The design of a social machine implies the use of electronics and, in many cases, radios—Wi-Fi, ZigBee, Bluetooth, ANT, 2G, 3G, 4G, LTE—to accomplish the network connection. As a result, you will need to contend with these issues. As I mentioned, even the biggest, most successful electronics companies (yes, even Apple) stumble over these exact obstacles. So don't feel like these lessons apply only to the naive and/or underfunded. But my hope is that by printing large versions of these and hanging them on your wall or tattooing them on your chest, you won't forget to at least consider them as you start and make your way through the design and production steps for your product. Social machines are awesome. Hardware is hard. See Lesson 1. ☺)

How Do I Make My Product Social?

As we saw in the earlier examples of weather stations versus wheelchairs, some products are easier than others to conceptualize as social machines. Sometimes the reasons are technical: It's simpler imagining a product that already has some sort of electronics in it as a connected node on a network. For example, imagining a refrigerator on the Internet is easier than imagining, say, a skateboard. But both can benefit from the connection. Other times, it feels like whole categories of products, market verticals, are more likely candidates for connectedness. For instance, it's fairly obvious why connecting health and medical devices to the Internet would provide enormous benefits. It's less clear why connecting living room furniture to social networks would be valuable. But just because one category seems less natural than another does not mean it should be discarded.

Following are some common product categories for social machines (but everything can be social!):

- Autos, trucks, and so on—basically anything with wheels
- Health/wellness—includes mHealth, athletic devices, disease management, drug compliance

- Safety/security—personal and premise safety, alarm systems

- Home—sometimes called smart home or home automation

- Financial—pay-as-you-go models

- Retail—social vending, digital signage, point of sale

- Energy—smart meters, solar

One way to help unlock the discussion for products that don't seem like natural candidates for connectedness is to stop looking at the situation from the perspective *of the product*. View it, instead, from the point of view *of the network*. Take the skateboard as an example. As a product designer, it would be easy to get stuck asking the question, "What sort of benefit would the skateboard get from being connected to the Internet?" The better question is, *"What sort of benefit would the network get from being connected to the skateboard?"* The first approach is product-centered. The latter one is centered on the community—a social entity. With that lens in place, the discussion shifts. The skateboard is not an isolated piece of fiberglass with wheels; it's a network node contributing data to a community. It's a social peer. All of the things we've discussed in this section could become relevant on the network both to the skateboard's actual owner and to others in the entire skateboarder community—local and global. It's a remarkably energizing perspective for designers.

Once you've convinced yourself of your new product's *social value*, you need to move from what and why to the practical and actionable *how*. Following are some of the key considerations you'll need to keep in mind as you think about the best ways to participate.

Many design decisions need to be made based on one of the business approaches I introduced in Chapter 11—retrofit versus built-in. Each approach drives a slightly different process of

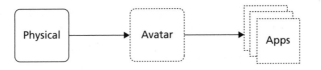

Figure 14.1   The Three Components of Social Machine Design

discovery and planning. But before I discuss the design consider-ations that each approach requires, I will present an overview of the main design points that affect all social machine design.

A "clean sheet of paper" approach to designing a social machine would need to take into account the three components, or aspects, of the design illustrated in Figure 14.1—the physi-cal device itself, its avatar's characteristics, and the services that will be offered, which can sometimes define the user interaction model as well. In addition, each of the three components needs evaluation in light of the three distinct customer types: primary customer, developer, and developer's customer.

I will go through each component separately to provide more detail on the major issues you need to consider. This is by no means an exhaustive guide. My goal is to make you aware of the most critical moving pieces included in each component so that you can feel educated about the choices you need to make in the areas in which you need to acquaint yourself more thor-oughly. To that end, the Resources section at the back of this book provides more useful information to help you continue your exploration.

The Physical Design

To a product developer today, this is obviously the most familiar component of social machine design, so I will focus only on the unique social machine elements that are important to consider when embarking on any project.

Where's the Brain? There's a serious debate right now concerning where the "smarts" for connected devices should reside. By *smarts*, I mean the computational resources—the computer or CPU—necessary to run application code. We touched on this issue in Part II when we were discussing the weather station design. Because social machines require application code running *somewhere*, this is an important topic. There are pros and cons for each approach, so it's important to understand each one. Let's break the options down:

- **Option 1:** The CPU could be included in the device itself. Using this approach, the product should have, all in one place, everything necessary to operate successfully alone and on a network. It is, in essence, a product with a computer at its core. This approach gives the designer the most control over the user experience, but it may introduce unacceptable cost and complexity increases. It also means additional power requirements.

- **Option 2:** We could leverage the "smarts" that already exist in the *smartphone* users carry (and have paid for). With this approach, the only thing the product designer needs to do is build in enough computing capability to connect to the phone via either a cable, Bluetooth, or similar short range radio. There is no need to include a full-fledged CPU in the design. With this approach, the connected device is a peripheral to the smartphone because the application runs on the phone's computer and not on the connected device. This helps keep the cost and complexity of the design low, but it requires a smartphone connection to execute its social functions. Today, only about half of the mobile customers in the United States have smartphones (although that number is growing quickly), so this requirement may be unacceptable for your target market.

- **Option 3:** We could use the power of cloud computing. In this model, the computational resources necessary for running the application reside on a server on the Internet, aka "the cloud." For example, you could use Amazon's Elastic Compute Cloud, or EC2, for this function. The connected device can, like in Option 2, be seen as a peripheral connected to the server via a network connection of some type. And like in Option 2, the connected device needs no CPU but only enough horsepower to open, manage, and close a network connection. This is a great approach if you know that you will always have a reliable network connection, and—if the use case requires wireless connectivity—adequate power to keep the connection up and running properly.

What's the right approach? Like everything else in life, it depends. At the end of the day, it's about finding the right balance between cost, function, form factor, and customer requirements. Is the use case mobile or stationary? How long does the device need to continue working on one battery charge? Does it require real-time streaming data from the device back to some centralized management center, or is it more like one update a minute? Are security and privacy of paramount importance? These are some of the crucial questions you need to ask when considering where to put the smarts for your social machine.

Network Connection

The next foundation stone for any social machine is its network connection, or how it will communicate on a network. There's no *social* in social machines without this capability. For networking options you have two choices: wired and wireless. They each have their strengths and weaknesses. Neither is better than the other. It truly depends on the design goals and the needs of the customer.

Currently, wireless is the trendier option. Who wants to deal with cables? But wireless introduces variables into the mix that may conflict with the product requirements. For example, if the device is meant to support health-related activities in, say, a hospital, the only option may be a wired connection because of the environment's twin sensitivities: data privacy and radio emissions. A wired solution may also be required when high speed and absolute reliability are required. The point isn't the technology per se. The point is to get the device on the network, to make it social.

If you choose a wired approach, the options are fairly straightforward, the most common approach being the standard RJ-45 (sometimes called an Ethernet) jack and cable. There are other, more esoteric choices, such as Ethernet-over-USB, but my recommendation is to stick with the standards. Otherwise, you will rack up serious expenses both creating and then supporting your custom approach (think about the new Apple iPhone5 Lightning connector as an example). The one issue with RJ-45 is it's a big connector, which requires some additional support circuitry to run properly. So designers going for the slimmest, sveltest design may resist this option. But if a wired connection provides the required features, then RJ-45 is the way to go.

Now, let's talk about the wireless options. If you've decided to endow your product with a wireless connection (or connections), then there are many things to consider. It's a complex field and sometimes difficult to know what the best option is. This is one area of product design where I feel all three lessons I listed earlier apply in spades. How you approach the selection of radios, how they are designed into the product, and how they will be used by the applications all have tremendous bearing on the success of your product. This is one reason there are firms that specialize in nothing but wireless product design (see the Resource section for more information). In fact, this may be a good solution for some organizations. But *how* it gets implemented doesn't absolve you from the responsibility of choosing the right approach to begin with. To avoid lots of words and potentially opaque descriptions, I've decided to construct a summary level listing of the various options, their strengths and weaknesses, and when and when not to include them in a design (Figure 14.2). This approach isn't perfect, but it should give you enough information to be dangerous.

Power

The other major question revolves around power—not only how much is required, but what its source will be. Besides the normal line and battery alternatives, is there the opportunity to use solar, wind, or some other source (nuclear perhaps)? Will the device be mobile or stationary? Mobility is a wonderful thing, and lots of target markets require it. But it comes at a cost, literally, at both the design and production levels.

The primary issue for mobile devices at the design phase is battery life: For how long must the device be able to perform its main functions on a single charge? The answer to this will drive all kinds of other decisions: battery size, material (lithium ion, alkaline, carbon-zinc, lead acid), and cost, as well as whether to use something off the shelf or build a custom solution. The second critical question is how the batteries will get replaced or charged. It's much easier to design a product with replaceable batteries, but there are trade-offs. Generally, lithium ion batteries (the kind that come built into most devices that you charge) hold a charge for much longer. The issue, though, is you'll need to build charging circuitry into your product. This isn't necessarily complicated. It just adds cost. But replaceable batteries introduce environmental costs because batteries are rarely disposed of properly. It's important to understand the technologies and how they affect your design and its use.

If you remember our wheelchair example, you *could* design a social machine with RFID tags that did not include a power source at all. But this would be only half the equation—half a

Network Type	Good For ...	Speed	Range	Power Requirements	Need Certification?	Comments
Wi-Fi	In building networks Campus and/or neighbourhood network	High	Medium	High but getting better	No	Most popular Low cost Quickly improving
2G cellular	Non-real-time applications	Slow	Nationwide	High	Yes	Good for certain apps but getting phased out by carriers
3G cellular	Good overall	Medium	Nationwide	Medium	Yes	Expensive radios
4G/LTE cellular	Best of real-time, low-latency-required applications	High	Nationwide	Medium	Yes	Expensive
ZigBee	In building	Slow	Limited but messages can jump between nodes to get to destination	Very low	No	Solid integrated software stack
ANT	In building, near field	Slow	Limited but messages can jump between nodes to get to destination	Very low	No	Popular choice for sports
Bluetooth	In building, in-vehicle, near field	Medium	Low	Medium, getting better	No	Ubiquitous in phones; tricky to program and use

Figure 14.2 Wireless Connection Types

social machine. You would still need a "dispenser" to complete the solution, a way to connect to the network. If you're planning on selling your product into an environment that could provide this type of connectivity, you're in luck. Your design could remain far simpler.

Input/Ouput, or I/O

The input/output (I/O) features of a product are, in many ways, what makes the product a product at all. It's all the stuff we physically interact with on the product itself: the display screen, buttons, knobs, sliders, and switches. It's the speakers, microphones, and keyboards. But it's also the things we might not interact with but that greatly influence the user experience: accelerometers (rotates the display on your smartphone from portrait to landscape), GPS (location finding device), thermometers, gyroscopes, proximity sensors, and many others. What's most important about I/O from the standpoint of social machine design is that, in most cases, the majority of the services that will get consumed via the network connection are based on these features. If you remember the weather station example, the temperature, barometric pressure, and humidity *sensors*, the unit's physical I/O, became, via the network, temperature, barometric pressure, and humidity data *services* that could be consumed from anywhere.

It's not hard to imagine a scenario in which you might include an I/O function that has no material value to the primary customer but has plenty of it for the developer and the developer's customer. This idea is not as nutty as it may sound. Your mobile phone has features on it that are invisible to you but are important to the carrier and other third parties that manage the provisioning, authentication, and remote monitoring of your phone on a network. Thinking about what the possibilities are in the design phase is important.

The ideal social machine should present all of its I/O features on the network so that other applications can access them to build new value. So as you chart out the features you think your product should have for your primary customers, seriously consider what additional features and functions could be added that would appeal to the other two types.

Avatar Design

Everything we've discussed so far has to do with the physical side of the equation. In that respect, we haven't broken too much new ground. Now let's explore the opposite side, which, frankly is more important for this discussion because it's what bequeaths everything I've introduced as social on the product. This is the layer that defines, controls, and supports the characteristics I call the social seven. Choosing the right tools and frameworks for supporting the product features and functions you intend to include is critical. There are plenty of choices, and which ones you choose depends on many variables. I've included more details on each in the Resources section at the back of this book. Keep in mind that the activity in this space is high and growing quickly. New tools and applications that focus on addressing the unique challenges of social products are emerging all the time.

I recognize that this component probably holds the most mystery for product designers and developers, so I will spend some time explaining why I introduced it and why it's a necessary ingredient in any social machine design. You will see that it's not as complicated as it may appear.

Whether you know it our not, you already have an avatar you use every day. It's your phone number. If you have more than one, then you have multiple avatars. As we discussed in Chapter 8, your phone number is an absolutely unique way of identifying yourself on a network. Actually, to be precise, it's a way of uniquely identifying your *phone* on the network (someone other than you could always answer it!). So when I pick up my phone and dial your number, my goal is to talk to you. But here's what actually occurs to make that happen (simplified):

- My phone requests the attention of the network (dial tone).

- My phone relays your unique identifier to the network management system packaged up with mine.

- If the phone number is valid (and you've paid your bill), the system sends your phone a signal that causes it to ring.

- You hear it and accept the call. This causes the system to connect your phone to mine over the network—basically connecting our unique IDs—our avatars.

- Our call commences.

Seems straightforward. We all know this is how it works. But let me point out something that usually just goes by without any notice. I didn't call your phone. I called a central hub controlled by the carrier that then called your phone. Or put another way, my avatar called your avatar over the network. The central management hub did all the routing. The phones then converted that avatar activity into a real, physical interaction. That's a critical step in understanding how avatars work with social machines—the physical device presents its avatar on a network so that it can interact with other avatars. How that avatar is designed is up to you.

But why is an avatar necessary? Why can't I just connect to my social machine over the network with my browser? You can, but we need to unbundle that sentence to figure what it takes to do it technically.

On the World Wide Web, when you point your browser to a specific URL, a central facility running a service called DNS (Domain Name System) performs what's called a lookup that translates what you typed in characters—for example, www .yahoo.com—into a bunch of numbers called an IP address. This is the unique identifier for the Web server hosting the information your URL points to. It's the equivalent of looking up someone's name in a phone book and using the telephone number to reach him or her. Once the lookup is complete, the system connects your browser to the targeted Web server and creates what's called a session, the equivalent of two phones connecting on a call. This is your own communication channel with the Web server, and it will respond to your inputs accordingly—mouse clicks, form submissions, and so on. The key point is there is a *central facility* that does all the routing between your browser and the Web servers.

So far so good. A Web server's IP address is its *phone number* on the Internet. Where does it get that number? From the same central facility that does all the routing (it's actually a little more convoluted than that, but that's not important for this discussion). But obtaining an IP address is not as straightforward as it may seem, especially if what you're trying to put on the Internet is not a Web server. It gets more complicated still if you want to use a Wi-Fi and/or cellular network for your network. It can get confusing, so I'll try to lay it out as simply as possible.

The main problem, and cause for much of the complexity, is there are no more IP addresses available. I know it sounds impossible, but when the original designers of the Internet developed the current addressing scheme, called IPv4, they didn't envision the World Wide Web and its explosion of servers and associated network connections (IPv4 only has about 4.3 billion unique IP addresses available). As a result, the pool of unique IP addresses created under this scheme has been exhausted. That's the bad news. The good news is a whole new addressing scheme, called IPv6, is rapidly coming online and should be the standard method of IP addressing in a couple years. This new scheme would allow for 4.8×10^{28} IP addresses *per person!* I think we'll be in good shape. But until then, we have to deal with the limitations of IPv4.

Here's an example of the complexity in action. Say I have a desktop computer at home that I'd like to connect to directly over the Internet. My home has a Wi-Fi router connected to a cable modem, which, in turn, connects to my cable company, which provides Internet access to my house. If I can set up my computer with an IP address, this shouldn't be a problem, right? Given everything I've said so far, it makes sense to think that, but it's not that straightforward. In reality, the actual IP address resides with my Wi-Fi router, which then splits up its use among all the devices in my home that connect to it. There are good reasons to do this—security being the primary one. The Wi-Fi router acts as a type of firewall prohibiting other unknown computers from attaching directly to your computer and potentially stealing or destroying data, spreading viruses, or damaging it in some way. The downside is you can't access your computer directly from outside this firewall.

This problem has created major business opportunities for companies able to solve it. There are many that provide solutions, but one of the most successful has been LogMeIn (logmein.com), which essentially allows you to access your desktop computer from anywhere on the Web, even if it's behind a Wi-Fi firewall. How do they do it? LogMeIn has developed a software application that you download to the computer you want to access. When you run this application, it connects to a special LogMeIn server in the cloud that then acts as your computer's proxy *outside* of your Wi-Fi router/firewall. When using LogMeIn, you're not actually accessing your computer directly. You're accessing LogMeIn's service, which is, in turn, communicating with your computer. The LogMeIn server creates an *avatar* of your real computer by communicating with it over the special connection established from the software on your computer.

The same problem exists with mobile phone networks. The lack of available IP addresses means that our phones do not come with one. Instead your phone is identified on its network using network-proprietary codes. You *can* request an IP address, but they are very expensive. And like the Wi-Fi example, for security's sake, it is sometimes better to not be directly on the Internet.

But for use cases that require establishing a direct IP connection with a mobile phone, the options are limited. Mobile carriers are jealous of their limited bandwidth and monitor its usage carefully. As a result, there are no companies like LogMeIn for cell phones. However, there are many mobile application companies that use similar techniques to enable applications that share data—some of the most popular being game developers who create games like Words with Friends (www.wordswithfriends .com), a game that supports multiple users playing a Scrabble puzzle-like game in real time with one another. Avatars are the key to these applications working as well.

These networking issues are becoming more and more pressing as the excitement being generated by the Internet of Things threatens to flood the Internet with millions, if not billions, of new devices all in need of IP connectivity. For social machines, the connection model requires a setup much like LogMeIn's.

When thinking about your social machine on a network, you have choices to make. Will you expose every I/O element or only a couple? Will you let anyone access the device indiscriminately, or do you want to restrict it in some way? And if you allow access, does everyone have the same level of privilege? Do you want users to have the ability to give their devices network names? How will you manage users that have more than one of your device? What tools will you provide to help them administer them? All of the social seven characteristics require careful consideration because if you're successful users will expect the same from them as they do everyone/everything else in their social network. Your answers to how you want to present your social machine and how you want to control the interaction with it defines your avatar.

The avatar is also the foundation for the application programming interface (API). Recall that the API is the documented collection of services that developers use to access the data on your social machine. All of the social seven characteristics that you expose via the avatar should be documented in the API. There are platforms available today that make it easier to define, organize, and administrate device avatars and APIs. I provide details on a number of them in the Resources section.

Designing your avatar and API interface correctly is as important as the physical attributes, features, and functions that demand so much attention.

Applications

The last component of the social machine design equation is the piece that interacts with the outside world. This is the application layer. Without an application accessing it, a social machine is just a network-connected device waiting to share itself with the community. Applications can come from the builder of the social machine or from an external source. Given that two of the three customer types refer to third-party application development, designing the device to attract these groups is imperative to realizing its full potential.

Referring back to our discussion on where to locate the "smarts" for running the application, we encounter the next logical question: What programming languages and environments should be used to write these applications? As usual, it depends on the use case, customer requirements, and chosen runtime environment.

If you recall, there are three ways for social machines to utilize applications:

- Option 1—Run it on the device itself.

- Option 2—Run it on a smartphone or similar computing device connected locally.

- Option 3—Run it in the cloud.

Let's look at each in more detail.

- **Option 1:** Running an application on the device implies that a CPU and associated support resources (for example, RAM) have been included in the design. What programming language you use to write applications depends in large part on the speed and processing power of the CPU. The C and C++ languages are popular because they are fast, flexible, and compact. They are also tricky to write and debug. Higher-level languages such as Java, Python, and C# are good choices if the device can support running them. All of these languages have well-designed and documented tools (many of which are free) to make it easier to code. One important issue that designers need to address with devices that run their own applications is how the code is updated on the device over time. Critical software updates as well as general upgrades need to be easily applied and installed, ideally with little to no user interaction.

- **Option 2:** This approach is similar to Option 1 in that it is constrained in large measure by the power and capacity of the smartphone to which the social machine is connected. Applications must include new sections of code for establishing, maintaining, and managing this connection and gracefully handling disconnects, reconnects, and other related problems. The programming language selection is identical to that in Option 1, with the added condition that certain smartphone makers restrict certain development options. For example, Apple iPhones run only applications written in Objective C.

- **Option 3:** Running your application in the cloud offers the most choices for application development. Amazon's EC2 platform allows you to run applications in just about any language you choose. A cloud-based application model has another important advantage: You can run Web applications written in languages such as node.js, PHP, Ruby, and others. The main benefit of this is it opens up the world of social machine application development to a much larger audience of developers. More sophisticated languages such as Java and C# require well-honed programming skills, whereas Web-centric development environments are easier and more forgiving. As a result, the population of Web developers dwarfs that of the others. However, to deploy this option, you need a specialized, always-connected operating environment.

There are two more important design issues to consider. They revolve around the business models I introduced in the prior section—retrofit and built-in. Each approach presents its own design advantages and disadvantages. But both require thinking through all the steps presented in this chapter.

RETROFIT MODEL

In Chapter 11, I introduced two business model types: Retrofit and Built-in. Both are valid approaches to building a social machine-based business. Of the two, the retrofit approach is usually the faster and cheaper route because you can potentially take advantage of resources that already exist in the product being retrofitted. The disadvantage is you are modifying an existing product, which can introduce a variety of limitations. Following are some design considerations that should be kept in mind when designing a *retrofit* social machine. For clarity, I will call the product being retrofitted the *target* and the device being designed to attach to it the *black box*.

Technical Considerations

Resources

Does the *target* have useable/accessible resources that your *black box* could capitalize on?

For example:

Power: Is there an existing power source in the *target*? What are its specifications? How would it be accessed? Does accessing it compromise the main functions of the *target* machine?

I/O: Are there existing sensors and/or other I/O sources in the *target* that can be tapped into? How would they be accessed?

Data: Are there existing data streams that can be monitored and captured? For example, if the device sends information to a printer, could you tap into that easily and use it for some other purpose? Or could data about the target be easily detected and used? How would they be accessed?

Enclosures: Are there areas or voids within the *target* that could be used to enclose the *black box* and hold/protect it?

Mechanical/industrial design

If the *target* does not offer any enclosure possibilities, how will the *black box* be securely installed or attached?

Is user access required? If so, how will it be facilitated?

Does the *black box* add user interface components to the *target*? If so, how can this be accomplished in as unobtrusive way as possible?

Will the *black box* be visible to end users? If so, what are visual/aesthetic design requirements and objectives?

Electrical design

How secure must the installation be? What electrical design precautions are necessary to ensure that data are protected, specifically as it pertains to the installation of the *black box* in the *target*. There are many ways to handle hardware-based security, from computers that boot up securely to tamper-proof encryption key stores (more than I can delve into here). Make sure you have a clear understanding of what's required and choose the appropriate approach.

Special Note: There is something imporant that we have noticed in the years we've been designing and building solutions for our customers. There are industries that have developed special standard electrical interfaces that span manufacturers in that industry. For example, the auto industry has adopted an interface called OBD (stands for "On Board Diagnostics"). The interface includes a standardized physical connector that's installed in virtually every car made today (and has been since 1996). The interface also includes a standard electrical signaling protocol. As a result OBD represents a great starting point for anyone considering the retro-fit model in the automotive vertical. Similarly, many vending machines since 1995 have incorporated an interface called MDB (for Multidrop Bus) that, like OBD, incorporated a physical and electrical standard. The point is, an interface that you can use to span manufacturers' product lines within a given industy are great retrofit candidates.

BUILT-IN MODEL

The other approach we referred to earlier was the built-in model. This approach is simpler from the standpoint that the designer has full control of the outcome. However, because there are no resources to leverage, as in the retrofit model, the design needs to provide for all aspects of what's necessary.

Technical Considerations

The brain (called the CPU—basically a computer or microprocessor): Where will it live? As we discussed in Chapter 14, there are several options, each with its own pros and cons.

Networking: Wired or wireless? What does the user experience require? Remember wireless seems to always sing the siren song for designers but there are plenty of good reasons not to go in that direction—from power to spotty coverage to speed.

Power: Wall power or battery? Both? Obviously mobility will require certain design decisions, unless it's a vehicle where you could potentially tap into the power sources available coming from the main battery or engine.

Input/output (I/O): Represents everything that interacts with the real world—sensors, touch screens, speakers, buttons, and so on.

Manufacturing Considerations

Are you developing a consumer device? If so, the type of manufacturer you choose is critical and needs to have substantial experience successfully delivering into that market. Apple has spoiled us all with flawless execution. Of course, manufacturing quality and attention to detail is just as important with other types of devices (e.g., industrial) but consumer devices require a level of fit and finish that is unique (and challenging).

Are you targeting the mass market or the DIY (do it yourself) community? This will affect how you plan for certifications. In many cases, products designed specifically for the DIY, prototyping, and hacker communities may not require FCC certification.

Designing social machines is, in many ways, similar to designing other network-connected electronic devices. But there are key differences that need attention if the device is to truly achieve its social potential, mainly associated with computation and communication features/functions. I've covered the main points in this chapter and have included more information on the relevant tools and software platforms available to help with the process in the Resources section.

CHAPTER 15

Getting There from Here

I argued in the beginning of Part II that social machines are an inevitable result of our innate desire and need for abstraction. Put another way, they will simply be another rung in the ladder of our continual process of knowing. Our minds are bottomless pits of curiosity. Every tool we have ever built is in service of this basic motivation—"What if . . . ?" In a way, realizing that we are now at the cusp of designing and deploying machines with the computational and physical capacities to mimic so many human qualities, one can't help but draw an analogy to Adam—"So God created man in his own image." Is that the point of all this? I don't think I'm qualified to answer.

The point is we will get there. In fact, we've almost arrived already. The technical foundation stones have been laid. It's now up to us to make the best use of them. Social machines are an evolution of what exists today. The social aspect of product design is merely the recognition that our things need to take on new responsibilities—to us, to one another, and finally, to the environment. Marketers throw around the term *smart* a lot these days—so much so that it has lost most of its meaning. But a true social machine must be smart in the strictest sense. It must communicate and interact. It must insinuate itself and gain our trust. It must, because it can, speak in the voice of its designer. As such, an authentic social machine design must embody values. In the book *Human-Built World*, author Thomas Hughes says, "We can use technology to consciously and purposefully shape our ecotechnological world according to our wishes, if we realize that technology is complexly value laden and that we can embody our values in its creations."

Social machines will be considered smart not because of their hardware and software capabilities. They will be considered smart because they coexist and interact with us and our world in profoundly new, dare I say, intelligent ways.

The Earth is not getting any larger. But we are. The resources available to us on the planet are not expanding. But we are. The good news is we, as a global population, are getting more connected. This has allowed us to share information about our communities, our cultures, our countries, and ourselves with others in real time. This has resulted in an increasing worldwide awareness of the issues we face over the coming century. Like the explorers and Pilgrims of 300 years ago, we are starting to entertain the escapist fantasies of colonizing foreign "lands," although in this case we're talking distant planets, such as the moon, Mars, and maybe even a Jovian satellite, and they are far less inviting. And frankly, as a die-hard technologist, I am confident we will do those things. But that doesn't solve anything for all the folks left back here on the original mother ship.

Connectedness, I have tried to show, leads to good things real, tangible benefits for us and our world. In the same way that human connectedness has improved the human condition, social machine connectedness will likewise improve it further. Why? Because the variety and depth of information the machines in our lives can provide will help us make better decisions. Not only will we be more connected to one another, but we will be bound more closely to our environment, both local and remote. We will feel more empowered and capable of informed action. A social network composed of both human and machine intelligence will help us lead healthier lives, design the best products, and be more resourceful and efficient.

We are all connected in some fashion, even if just via our basic humanity. But we are also connected to the things we make. We and our tools are of a piece, yin and yang. Like everything we create, they are our responsibility. We share the Earth with one another *and* all our stuff. We remove resources from the ground, water, and air to build things and return them, unfortunately in the vast majority of the cases, back to Earth in a completely unreusable form. To quote Bruce Sterling "Shaping Things" again:

"The production methods currently used are not sustainable. They are large in scale, have long histories, and have been extensively researched and developed, but they can't go on in their present form. The status quo uses archaic forms of energy and materials that are finite and toxic. They wreck the climate, poison the populace and foment resource wars. They have no future."

The social machine concept represents a wide-open new field for innovation. The idea represents a step function in how we build, use, and share our tools to experience and manipulate the world. Like all other types of tools, there will be good ones and poor ones. The users will sort it all out. But if ever there was a time to join the fray and experiment, prototype, deploy, succeed, and fail with something new, now is that time. The world of connected humans but disconnected objects is quickly fading. As Buckminster Fuller eludes to in his quote, we need the designers to help show us the way.

PART V

Scenarios

Included in this section are a variety of use cases and scenarios that I think demonstrate not only what has happened and is happening in the world of social machines but also what's possible and promising in each of the selected vertical market segments. These examples highlight both the opportunities and challenges designers and organizations face when exploring this new direction, and they serve as great starting points for further thinking on the benefits of combining social attributes with physical objects.

CHAPTER 16

Smart Home

Let me start this scenario by playing the cynic. I have been in high-tech businesses my entire career, and there have been, for that entire time, two technologies that were always "about to be huge": artificial intelligence (AI) and home automation. These are technologies that, on the surface, make enormous sense. They promised all kinds of benefits, advantages, and conveniences. Your AI-enabled computer would become like HAL (from the movie *2001: A Space Odyssey*) and interact with you like a human. Your AI-fortified house would recognize patterns, predict situations, and provide bulletproof security. Home automation has been working on its own core concepts for decades. Wouldn't it be great if your alarm clock could talk to your coffeemaker so it would start to brew a fresh pot as soon as you got out of bed?! Or wouldn't life be easier if your lights all responded to you locking the front door? There have been many interesting ideas proposed and prototyped, but none have gone mainstream. Today you'd be hard-pressed to find much of anything home automation related at your local hardware store (though Lowe's did just introduce a product called "Iris," but as of this writing it's unclear if it will be a success).

Delving into the hows and whys of this situation is not the point of this scenario, but I will argue that when it comes to technologies focused on making homes more comfortable, safe, and efficient, adding a social layer to the mix will help significantly. Home automation solutions have long suffered from an addiction to proprietary, vertically integrated technology architectures that produce rigid, monolithic systems that are difficult to change and adapt to our very personalized living situations. As a result, they typically have either a lowest-common-denominator feel or an everything-but-the-kitchen-sink design (and cost).

A social machine approach to the challenges of home automation would open up the interfaces of the devices in the home and make them available for innovative new approaches and solutions to well-known problems. A set of open social interfaces would allow appliances to share data with energy management devices. As we saw in our social air conditioner example, once you start to recognize the benefits of sharing, it's difficult to accept any other approach.

As a good example of the promising work being done in this field, I will focus on a new West Coast–based start-up called Nest. Founded by Tony Fadell and Matt Rogers (both of Apple iPod and iPhone fame), Nest is attempting to bring new design thinking to the world of thermostats (yes, those normally clunky, ugly things that hang on your wall and control the interior temperature of your home). The mere fact that talented designers and engineers like Fadell and Rogers would find the market space attractive after spearheading the launch of some of the most famous electronic devices of all time should tell you something. Certainly, there is plenty of room for improvement when it comes to thermostat design. But I think it should be equally clear that that's not the end game for Nest. Their company's name actually says it all. They are interested in your home—the whole thing, not just its temperature. And their company is causing heartburn and hand wringing at every major home and building automation company in the world.

Their first product is what they call a learning thermostat. Unlike traditional thermostats that require you to program them using quirky, cumbersome, and VCR-like programming methods, the Nest device pays attention to how you set it, how you change it, and when. It records and stores this usage information so that it can start to make predictions on its own.

I am turned down to 50 degrees every night at 11 PM.

Every Saturday I trigger the air-conditioning unit to come on until the temperature reaches 68 degrees.

There are two good reasons for this approach. Obviously, eliminating the need to program the device is paramount, as this is usually a cumbersome, user-hostile activity. Give the Nest device time, and it will figure out how you want to run your house and comply. The second reason is to save money. A thermostat that has learned your patterns and "understands" what to do and when means you won't leave the house for the weekend with the heat still pegged at 75 degrees. You won't inadvertently keep the air-conditioning pumping all night long. Nest claims that using their device can save you up to 20 percent on your energy bill. That's not bad.

I can hear you thinking that all this is great but none of it is terribly social. But here's where that storyline begins. Soon after the release of its product, Nest launched the Nest Mobile app that allows you to control your new thermostat from anywhere. This assumes that you have Wi-Fi in your home and have successfully connected your device to it. So they've taken the important step of developing the interface needed to adapt their potentially lonely, isolated device into a more social gadget.

They've also done some advanced planning when you examine the innards of the thermostat itself. Soon after the device was made available to the public, a group of hackers (some professional, some not) decided to open it up and tear it down. The results were interesting and, I'm sure, cause for further anxiety from Nest's competitors. Embedded in each thermostat are a couple of things that are not touted on the website: a powerful ARM-based CPU capable of running applications and a low-speed (compared with Wi-Fi) ZigBee radio. We can assume the CPU is used to run the learning algorithms and other associated applications, but it's capable of executing far more complicated apps, too. The ZigBee radio has no documented use at the moment. But a quick review of the market segments where ZigBee has been popular will reveal—yes, you guessed it—home automation. With this combination of powerful CPU and ZigBee radio embedded in every Nest thermostat, it is not hard to imagine the product trajectory Fadell and team probably have in mind. Start with a successful thermostat that captures the hearts and imaginations of customers and developers everywhere. Get it installed in as many homes as possible as quickly as possible. Then open the system's application programming interfaces (APIs) to the third-party developers of the world and watch them flock to the platform and add all kinds of new value. If this approach sounds familiar, it should. It's exactly what Apple did with its iPhone.

If you recall, the iPhone had no developer program available at its debut. This caused a huge uproar, as everyone wanted the opportunity to write applications for it. But whether by intention or not, Apple waited. It managed to sell millions of iPhones before the official developer platform was launched. Coincidentally, and fortunately for Apple, this created what every developer craves—a large, captive market for their wares. It was now an easy calculation to fame and fortune: Sell your new $0.99 application to 3 million iPhone customers and retire early! I suspect Fadell and company have similar intentions.

But here is where the questions start, for me at least. Nest needs to make a decision.

Given their successful history at Apple, a company that has championed the concept of a totally closed and proprietary approach to development, will Fadell and Rogers follow that same path? Will they pursue the identical route every other home automation supplier has taken over the past 30 years and demand that customers buy everything from them or nothing at all? Will they insist that homes be "Nest homes" before customers and developers alike can truly benefit? Or will they let their devices become true social machines by allowing them to participate in the open community? If they do, then I think they have a much better chance of avoiding the fate that has befallen every other would-be home automation leader.

CHAPTER 17

Retail

There is now a whole new, emerging category of retailing called social retail. It includes a number of different areas, but in essence, you can summarize its arrival as a way for brick-and-mortar retailers to compete with Amazon. If you are a retailer of any kind, it's virtually impossible not to feel the competitive pressures posed by the online giant and those like it. I think most of us are already guilty of a behavior so prevalent it's received its own buzzword: showrooming. This is the name of the activity you engage in when you go into a brick-and-mortar retailer to check out in person a product you're interested in but then actually buy it online—while you're still in the store! Talk about a retail nightmare. You get all the cost but none of the revenue. It sort of sounds like it should be illegal.

The whole point of social retail is to take advantage of something no online retailer can touch: your physical presence. There isn't anything new about that. Retailers have always understood the importance of this fact. The whole science and practice of merchandising is based on this simple idea: Take advantage of the fact the customer is in the store—right now! What is new about social retail is the online component. Social networking and social media have given retailers the ability to reach customers in new ways. More important, though, these same tools have given customers the ability to spread the word of great retail experiences instantly. This ability, in theory, drives additional interest in the retailer as customers' social graphs get activated, inspiring new visits and business for the retailer. Online social networking sites such as Yelp, Foursquare, and OpenTable are helping drive this wave of interest with various degrees of success.

One often-overlooked component of this trend is the piece of connected hardware that is essential to its success—the smartphone you carry in your pocket or purse. Without this advanced piece of networked electronics, none of this would be possible. In many instances, its primary purpose is to serve as a GPS homing beacon for sites the user visits. In this way, online buying guides and portals can offer highly personalized and localized suggestions and promotions. In other cases, the smartphone is just a mobile Web browser giving users real-time access to relevant retail information. Most recently, the smartphone camera has catalyzed substantial excitement around the newfangled square bar code variant called the QR code. With a special application on your phone, you can easily scan a QR code, which, in turn, opens a Web browser that navigates to a specific URL (that's been encoded in the QR code). It's a neat trick because it capitalizes on the fact that you are in a specific location—standing in front of the QR code sticker!—while simultaneously connecting you to relevant online information or buying opportunities. This is the reason you see them popping up everywhere.

There are other innovative new opportunities being pursued as well. The first chapter of this book introduced you to the social vending machine—a connected device that combines the power of your retail presence with the marketing benefits of social networks. The machine itself represents the nexus of two worlds: one physical and the other virtual. It is at this point that you can trade your social capital for real capital—a Facebook Like for a tangible physical good.

Other interesting efforts are being pursued as well in the space. In April 2012 at the National Automatic Merchandising Association's One Show in Chicago, Pepsi announced the launch of its Social Vending System, a "state-of-the-art networked unit that features full touch-screen interactive vending technology, enabling consumers to better connect with PepsiCo brands right at the point of purchase."

This Social Vending System uses a different type of social currency than the Facebook Like. This machine allows users to gift a free beverage to any friend with a mobile phone. By simply entering the friend's name, mobile number, and short personalized message, users can send the free beverage gift, redeemable at any other Pepsi Social Vending machine. Users also have the option of recording a short video using the machine's built-in video camera. Recipients redeem their gift by entering a special code and, upon receiving their gift, can either thank the original sender by returning a gift of their own or pay it forward and send a beverage gift to another friend. Pepsi also included the innovative Random Acts of Refreshment feature, which lets users buy/gift drinks for complete strangers via any Social Vending System.

Not to be outdone, Coca-Cola developed the a mobile app Open Happiness (based on their latest marketing campaign of the same name) that works with vending machines in four cities in three separate countries—Buenos Aires, Cape Town, New York, and Mountain View. Using the application, Coca-Cola fans could send free Coke to anyone in any of the cities. In return, they get to watch a video of the recipients as they receive their free beverage and, hopefully, share in the joy of the gift.

Here's another one: BOS Ice Tea of South Africa developed the world's first Twitter-activated vending machine. In this case, free samples are dispensed from the machine in return for a user tweeting about the machine. Like the first example, users are trading social for physical capital.

COMPANY PROFILE

I had the chance to sit and speak with Peter Corbett, the cofounder and chief executive officer (CEO) of DC-based iStrategyLabs (istrategylabs.com). His firm does many things but has made social machine design, development, and deployment a core service offering, with an impressive collection of successes already under the team's belt. Here are a couple of great examples of their work.

(continued)

(*continued*)

THE GE SOCIAL FRIDGE

Built using a Vintage 1939 model refrigerator, iStrategyLabs designed a social machine interface that pops the fridge open once 10 people have checked into it via Foursquare. Making its debut at the South by Southwest (SXSW) 2012 conference in GE Garages (ge.com/garages/) pavilion, the Social Fridge was a big success.

THE FOURSQUARE SOCIAL COOLER

Like the GE Social Fridge, the Foursquare Social Cooler unlocks when the magic number of people check in on Foursquare. The prize? Cold beer!

What is great about both these examples is they adhere to a vision that is core to the success of social machines. These are connected devices that are not concerned with saving money for their owners/operators. The return on investment analysis, if anyone would ever decide to put one together, would not be based on achieving specific levels of operational efficiency. Rather the whole investment thesis for these machines hinges on returns based on things such as revenue generation, user interaction, and market awareness. The potential owners and operators of these social machines are less concerned with stocking levels. They are far more interested in the social engagement that the machines provide to users and their brand.

These innovative social machines are also great examples of how connected devices can participate seamlessly in a social network and interact in ways that users love. They require no new behaviors of their users. In this case, if you knew how to use Foursquare, you knew how to use this social machine. Checking in, which is a user behavior that *defines* Foursquare, was a simple and intuitive affair. But unlike a normal Foursquare check-in, which provides only digital feedback on the screen of your mobile phone, checking in to, say, the GE Social Fridge could actually unlock it, giving you a beverage. Your actions in digital space can now affect objects in your physical space, right where you're standing. Right now. It's a fascinating new interaction model that is entirely novel to most users. As a result, the impact is very high and the viral effect strong. The nice thing about this concept is it can be used in all kinds of scenarios. And the results don't have to be trivial. You could easily imagine an application where remote caregivers are capable of interacting with home-based electronics to ensure things were kept in order and not on all the time.

According to Corbett there is lots more where this came from. He mentioned himself, and his website confirms, that there are many, many opportunities out there for the social machines approach. Right now iStrategyLabs is working on a significant social vending machine project with Campbell. How cool would it be if you could take some of your Facebook "capital" and trade it for real capital—maybe not hard currency, but goods and services. I'm not sure what the details are, but I would guarantee that the vending machine will serve as the interface between new Campbell products and all the users of the machine. Campbell's intent is not to find a way to save money here. It is to improve the value of its brand with customers new and old, those folks who are looking for good reasons to try something new. Properly developed and deployed social machines are not like your grandfather's M2M. They are not remote assets in need of tracking. They are

(continued)

(continued)

newfangled smart brand ambassadors that can engage users and deliver messages in entirely new ways. They can change on a dime to respond personally to specific users and specific situations. Most important, they can engage and interact. The social aspect of the interactions creates a whole new set of opportunities for everyone in the value chain to innovate on top of—from the vending machine manufacturers to the operators and service/maintenance to the systems integrators and individual entrepreneurs. The social abstraction layer creates a green field opportunity for those brave enough to jump in.

These three examples are focused on a specific type of social machine—vending. But the same opportunities are available with other types of retail-related machines as well. For example, digital signs that interact with users offer many interesting possibilities. Equipped with cameras, facial recognition software, and other types of sensors, these devices provide platforms for many types of innovation.

Point-of-sale systems and kiosks are also great examples of machines capable of capitalizing on a customer's physical presence. Like vending machines, they offer intriguing possibilities to engage not just with users locally but with users *anywhere* in the community.

CHAPTER 18

Transportation

In my experience, the best examples of machines acting socially come from the least expected places. It reinforces a deeply held belief that I have about the origins of a real disruptive change. It's not always true. There are plenty of examples otherwise. But my bias is that the real new, new things rarely come from big companies. They come from determined individuals or small groups passionately pursuing a new idea in the cleared-out mythical Silicon Valley garage.

Occasionally, large companies get it right and form small entrepreneurial offshoots that are given the intellectual and financial freedom to pursue their vision. The original IBM Personal Computer, model 5150—the famous IBM PC—is a great case in point. Based in Boca Raton, Florida, the design team broke all the rules and developed an IBM product in one year, not the usual four. The rest is history.

Another way large companies try to act smaller and more nimble is to provide tools to independent groups in the hopes of benefitting from their innovation and out-of-the-box thinking. This scenario is a good example of exactly that.

Weather forecasting is a tricky business. It's also an expensive business. Today, forecasters rely on a combination of advanced geostationary satellites, a nationwide system of NEXRAD weather radars, and specialized Doppler radars installed at 41 of the major U.S. airports. In addition, they use weather balloons, airplanes, and dedicated weather data collection sites located in strategic areas around the country. Frustratingly, even with all this technology, no one can tell you with any certainty whether it's pouring rain on the piece of highway you are about to travel on. The nation's weather tracking and forecasting systems are fantastic tools for generalized reporting. They are less reliable for specifics. To answer the question about the rain situation on a highway, there's one obvious reliable source—the cars actually traveling on it.

Once you've convinced yourself that the cars driving on a road would be a great source of highly localized, real-time weather data, you now must figure out how to gather and share that information. To my knowledge, there are no cars cruising around today with built-in weather stations just ready for exploitation. We'll need to find another way. Luckily, some creative thinkers came up with a solution.

In 2012 Ford released the first version of a technology platform called OpenXC (www.openxcplatform.com), a set of open source hardware and software tools for allowing developers to write applications and build hardware for a variety of Ford vehicles. It was a tool kit for inspiring others to do cool things with their Ford cars and trucks, and it caught the attention of the folks at Weather Underground, an innovative company that publishes a weather-related Web portal (wunderground.com). They had a question. Could you, via the OpenXC platform, remotely access operating information about the windshield wipers? Could you determine whether they were on or not and at what speed they were moving? If the answer was yes, couldn't you logically deduce the presence of rain at that car's location? Furthermore, they reasoned, the quality of that data would be high because it would be validated by the driver. For example, if the car had an automatic rain sensor that activated the windshield wipers and the driver did *not* override it and turn them off, you could be fairly certain it was raining enough to matter. Conversely, if the car did not have an automatic system and the windshield wipers were on it, would be because the driver activated them—another good indication of the rain conditions where the car was located. Bottom line: Windshield wiper activity would provide high-quality, driver-corroborated data about localized weather conditions. Weather Underground could then take that data, mash it up with other sources of information, and present a map or other visualizations to users that offered a whole new level of granular forecasting.

However, recognizing that the data would be a great resource is different from actually getting your hands on it. This is particularly true when the car is moving, potentially at high speed, down a road. To help explore the possibilities, Ford has turned to innovative communities of tinkerers, makers, and students for inspiration and answers, working with US-based groups and universities as well as international organizations like the prestigious Indian Institute of Technology in Bangalore. It is an on-going project, but to-date the results have been extraordinarily encouraging.

Briefly, the OpenXC platform is a way to safely tap into the operational information of a Ford vehicle by connecting to what's called the OBD-II port. This is a standard interface that just about every vehicle has had installed since 1996. It is normally used by car manufacturers, dealers, and service stations to access the operational status and metrics of your car. You pull into the garage, and someone wheels over the diagnostics computer, plugs into the OBD-II port, and gets an instant readout on the health of your vehicle. As it turns out, one of the signals that can be routed over this interface is windshield wiper activity. And OpenXC makes it easy for developers to get access to that information.

OpenXC also includes an interface to add USB peripheral devices to the system as a way to enhance the functions of the car—in essence, extending its hardware feature set. In this case, the addition of a USB-based 3G wireless modem (sometimes called a dongle) would solve the problem of transmitting the windshield wiper data to an outside database so that it could be used. A USB-based Bluetooth interface could also be used to pair the OBD-II connector to the driver's phone, which would have then served as the conduit to the outside world.

OpenXC is a terrific example of a social machine's potential. It utilizes all the concepts introduced in this book and demonstrates how powerful the inclusion of machine-originated data can be. In this case the windshield wiper information is not only useful but could help save lives. The sharing of simple operational data produces positive results and measurable benefits for the entire community. The task of weather data collection becomes crowdsourced. Combining this information with the more advanced, but more generalized, weather data coming from the satellites, radars, and balloons could present forecasters and end users with a considerably more accurate and predictable picture of the weather—courtesy of social machines!

For another example of a company taking advantage of the standard OBD-II ports available on vehicles, you can check out Mavizon (mavizon.com). Mavizon has built a platform similar to OpenXC that includes a hardware interface that connects to your car and, in turn, communicates with your smartphone. Its power is in its simplicity, and its goal is to allow third-party developers to write applications to improve every aspect of owning and operating a car.

CHAPTER 19

Finance

I have to admit that when thinking about all the potential benefits social machines could bring to the world, finance and finance-related products did not immediately occur to me. I think the reason is because I was hung up on the idea that a product is a physical, tangible thing, which of course it isn't. But when you're thinking about machines, your mind tends to think atoms. I was straightened out when I saw this quote on a subway poster for Progressive Insurance:

> Over $70 million already saved with Snapshot! You could save up to 30% EXTRA for YOUR good driving!

We've already spent time in Chapter 10 going through the whole Progressive Insurance story so I won't repeat it here. But the poster headline listed above caught my attention less because I'm looking for a good deal on auto insurance and more because I recognized that you could pretty easily swap out "good driving" with other equally compelling words. Usage-based insurance would seem to make sense for lots of people and businesses since it sharpens the tools used to price insurance premiums and makes insurance fairer.

Take health insurance for example and replace "good driving" with "healthy living."

Wouldn't it make sense to pay less for health insurance if you lived a healthy lifestyle? It would seem to fall right in line with what Progressive has done with automobile coverage. Turns out there is a ton of interest and debate about the topic—everything from what are the best models to is it even legal. There are models that pay you for taking your prescription drugs[1] and others that reward you for staying healthy and submitting to biometric

---

[1] http://www.nytimes.com/2010/06/14/health/14meds.html?_r=0

tests and stress counseling.[2] Plenty of insurance companies offer incentives to stay healthy because it's a win-win proposition.

Given the interest, it's not hard to understand why a company like United Healthcare launched its $60,000 Open Innovation Challenge at the 2013 Consumer Electronics show. Here the description from their press release:

"[The] open innovation initiative . . . invites people around the world to submit new solutions that will enhance the health system and help people lead healthier lives."

It's equally understandable that they launched this initiative at one of the world's largest electronics trade shows—there is incredible interest in using smart, connected devices to help individuals, doctors, care givers, and health-related organizations to better monitor health, provide real-time feedback, and promote healthier living. In fact, there were many new health and fitness tracking products on display. But we are only scratching the surface of what's possible. Creating truly *social* health, medical, and wellness devices will bring a whole new level of innovation to this field and help increase both the quantity and quality of shared data needed to radically affect positive change. Social devices will empower communities to better take care of themselves, relying less on large, often cumbersome central providers and improve the collective health of all their members.

Health device makers could easily provide secure interfaces to their products that allow remote access to authorized users. The devices themselves could post relevant information to insurance company databases or social networks. Third-party developers could offer applications that simultaneously help users live

---

[2]http://www.seattlemag.com/article/health-rewarding-work

healthier, more active lives and provide insurance companies with the data they need to keep rates low.

You could even imagine pay-as-you-go insurance for pets with connected collars, health monitors, trackers, and so on, providing the required data to owners and insurance companies alike.

The point here, like in every scenario in this section, is to demonstrate how social machines are not only creating an environment for an improved standard of living but creating solid business opportunities as well. Expect to see many more examples of this in the future as we more and more come to rely on social machines to provide the necessary supporting data.

CHAPTER **20**

Health and Wellness

Imentioned in Part I that I have personally spent time focusing on how health issues can be addressed in new ways, not so much with technology, but with a community approach to care and support. I've come to call it "people taking care of people," or finding ways and methods to help us take better care of one another. My belief is that big health-related companies—insurance, pharma, hospitals—will continue to play a vital role. But in the same way that sites such as PatientsLikeMe (patientslikeme.com) are finding ways to use the Internet to connect people with similar conditions so that they can share knowledge and experiences, there is a mountain of innovation waiting to happen by sharing other types of information as well.

This scenario is based on work we did a couple years ago that revolved around helping companies that focus on elder care provide a higher standard of attention and quality of service. The solution was based on connected devices of various sorts, which I describe next, and a back-end server that kept track of it all, providing reports, analyses, and other relevant content useful for managing and operating an elder care facility. What was not explored at the time was the power of social networking in helping improve care. I will add how it could have dramatically altered, for the better, various aspects of the project and improved the outcome.

Elder care facilities have many configurations, but the one we worked on was composed of modest apartments that afforded a fairly independent living style for the people living there. They could come and go as they pleased (unless there was a medical reason they couldn't). They could also tap into the support services offered by the facility to the degree that they needed them. As a care-related facility, the staff wanted to provide high-quality service on a very individualized basis, ensuring that their customers received the most useful and effective assistance when and if they needed it, 24 hours a day, seven days a week.

One interesting challenge with the apartment approach is everyone is different. Apartment A may be home to a person with a congestive heart condition. Apartment B may be home to a woman with Alzheimer's disease, and apartment C to a diabetic. And to make matters worse, there is normally (unfortunately) a high degree of turnover, so apartment A may have its specific setup for that occupant in place for only a couple of months. Last, the medical systems that would get installed in each apartment to help monitor and assist both the person living there and his or her caregivers were all completely proprietary, closed, and highly vertically integrated so that they worked great within their sphere of use—for example, a glucometer testing the sugar level in a patient's blood—but did not "play nice" with the other devices in the apartment. This closed approach affects many things, which we will discuss later. But perhaps the most obvious is that proprietary health systems that focus on highly specific conditions can be terrific at addressing the needs of people with those conditions, but for everyone else who touches those systems, the costs are high. Perhaps the best example was provided by talking to the nurses who worked in the facility. It turns out that because each apartment usually housed a person with a different situation than that of their neighbors, the systems installed to monitor them varied from apartment to apartment. And because privacy issues are of paramount importance, sometimes operating these devices and machines would require a log-in or hardware access key. The nurses therefore ended up running around with a catalog of log-ins and used whatever combination was necessary in each apartment. Naturally, this was an administrative nightmare that the facility hoped to improve.

As a result, the facility's management had a hard time putting a complete health picture together for each individual because the data from the various devices used in each apartment to track the important health and medical metrics were hard to correlate and summarize in meaningful ways.

The goal was to create a modular hardware system, based on the Bug Labs platform, that would allow the facility to install exactly what was needed—sensors, monitors, and so on—in each apartment. It could also quickly change the installation to accommodate either a new condition or situation to be monitored. Best of all, the information coming from these newly installed devices would be based on a standard format, so it would be easy to compare apples to apples across apartments and even across disease types. The information produced by the devices would be collected at a central server and used to produce helpful Web-based dashboards for everyone—the occupant, the caregivers, and management.

But how do you make it *social?*

According to a June 2012 Forrester report on "Digital Seniors," 60 percent of U.S. seniors are online, which amounts to approximately 20 million people. And of those, close to 50 percent have Facebook accounts. Those are big numbers. These seniors are using social media to share their lives and connect with communities. If you combine this type of social networking activity with the open, modular information sharing solution described earlier, you get the perfect environment for social machine innovation. As I discussed in my Hacking Health example (in Part I), by integrating health- and wellness-related data with online communities that include family members, friends, doctors, nurses, caregivers, companions, and other relevant people, you create a virtuous dynamic—people taking care of one another—looking out for those they love and care about. It would not take much for the makers of all the health monitors used in these facilities to create social machines out of their existing product offerings—in fact, go review the retrofit model we discuss in Part IV! This approach would also help unleash the creativity and energy of the global developer community, bringing to the world of health and wellness a level of interest and activity that it is currently sorely lacking. Although we focused on elder care facilities in this example, there isn't a corner of the health world that the social machines movement will not touch.

PART VI

Resources

Resource	Specialty	URL
Contract Manufacturers		
Circuitco Electronics, LLC	Complex builds, TI processors, Low to medium volume	http://circuitco .com/wordpress/
Edmond Marks	High mix, Low volume, Quality build cycle	http://www .edmondmarks .com/
Solutions Manufacturing	Medium to large volume, In house part suppliers, Test rigs	http://www.solu tionsmfg.com/
Surya Electronics	Prototypes, Low volume, Off shore high volume	http://www.sury aelectronics.com/
Innovative Global Solutions	Local representatives, Overseas manufacturing, High volume, Full production	http://www.innova tiveglobalsolutions .com/

Resource	Specialty	URL
Design Firms		
Mistral Solutions	Hardware, Software design engineering	http://www.mistralso lutions.com/
ECCO	Product design	http://www.eccoid .com/
IDEO	Product Design	http://www.ideo.com/
BERG Team	Networks of physical things	berglondon.com
Bug Labs, Inc.	Product development: Hardware, Software engineering, Cloud platform/tools	http://www.buglabs .net
Y Studios	Design consultancy	http://www.ystudios .com/
iStrategyLabs	Strategists, designers, Developers	http://istrategylabs .com/
Housings		
Copesetic Inc.	Fast prototype housings, Urethane, SLA, SLS, CNC	http://copeseticinc .com/
Solid Concepts, Inc.	3D prints, Rapid prototyping, Low volume, High volume overseas production	https://www.solidcon cepts.com/
Spectrum Plastics Group	High quality, Quick turn tooling	http://www.spectrum plasticsgroup.com/
Parts Distributors		
DigiKey	Parts supplier, Kits	www.digikey.com
Mouser	Parts supplier, Kits	www.mouser.com
Arrow	High volume parts supplier, Kits	www.arrow.com
Spark Fun	DIY kits and gadgets, Community help	http://www.sparkfun .com/

Resource	Specialty	URL
Parts Distributors (Continued)		
Seeed Studios	Open hardware facilitator—from kits to overseas production	http://www.seeedstudio.com/depot/
Adafruit	DIY components, Kits and gadgets, Community leadership, Help	http://adafruit.com/
PCB Manufacturers		
Sunstone	Quick turn, Low volume, CAD design SW	http://www.sunstone.com/
Advanced Circuits	Quick turn, High volume, Assembly options	http://www.4pcb.com/
Hallmark Circuits	Quality, Speed	http://hallmarkcircuits.com/
Electrotek	Quality, High volume, Low cost, Design review	http://boards4u.com/
Cables		
C&M Corporation	Cable assemblies, Coil cord assemblies	http://www.cmcorporation.com/
CSI Electronics	Custom hand built, Low volume, Fast service	http://csielectronics.com/
ICT	Custom large volume	http://www.intcomptech.com/
Communities		
IOT	Research and forecasting of what the world will become	http://www.theinternetofthings.eu/
Web of Things Community	Community tinkerers	http://www.webofthings.org/

Resource	Specialty	URL
Communities (Continued)		
Tech Shop	Tools, SW, Space to build anything	http://www.tech shop.ws/
NYC Resistor	Hacker community in NYC	http://www.nycre sistor.com/

Social Machine Cloud Platforms

Systems for coordinating the messaging between connected devices. Support for the Social Seven and Avatar interaction.

Resource	Specialty	URL
Bug Labs Swarm	Turns any connected device into a collection of web APIs	http://developer .bugswarm.net/ index.html
Cosm	Connect devices and apps, Exchange data and ideas	https://cosm.com/
Digi	Any app, anything, anywhere	http://www.idigi .com/
Evrything	Managed applications to help make products smart	http://www .evrythng.com/
Logica—Now CGI	Innovation, Flexibility, Security, Performance	http://www.cgi.com/ en/cloud

Integrated Development Environments

Resource	Specialty	URL
ThingWorx	M2M/IoT application development platform	http://www.thing worx.com/
Axeda	Cloud-based service and software for managing devices	http://www.axeda .com/
ILS Technology	Simply and securely enables M2M services	http://www.ilstech nology.com/

Resource	Specialty	URL
Wireless System Design		
Delta Mobile	Wireless design and manufacture	http://www.del tamobile.com/index .html
Connected Development	Wireless M2M design	http://www.connect eddev.com/
Certification Labs		
7 Layers	FCC, PTCRB	http://www.7layers .com/#!/certification
SGS	Complete testing services	http://www.sgs group.us.com/en/ Service-by-Type- Path/Certification .aspx
Nemko	EMC, R&TTE	http://www.nemko .com/
MET Labs	EMC, EMI, Wireless and RF testing	http://www.metlabs .com/
Compliance Testing	FCC, IC, CE, EMC, EMI, RF	http://www.compli ancetesting.com
Cetecom	PTCRB, BT, LTE	http://www.cetecom .com

Books

Smart Things: Ubiquitous Computing User Experience Design	Author: Mike Kuniavsky
Designing Interactions	Author: Bill Moggridge
The Design Of Design: Essays From A Computer Scientist	Author: Frederick P. Brooks

INDEX